# TASTE
## *of*
# CHINA

*Deh-Ta Hsiung*

# TASTE
## *of*
# CHINA

*Deh-Ta Hsiung*

Photography by Edward Allwright

INDEX

This edition first published by
Acropolis Books
Desford Road, Enderby
Leicestershire, LE9 5AD

This edition exclusively
distributed in Canada by
Book Express, an imprint of
Raincoast Books Distribution Limited
112 East 3rd Avenue
Vancouver
British Columbia V5T 1C8

ISBN 1 873762 51 8

Distributed in Australia by
Treasure Press

Editorial Director: Joanna Lorenz
Project Editor: Lindsay Porter
Photographer: Edward Allwright
Designer: David Rowley Design
Stylist: Maria Kelly

Printed and bound in Singapore

Recipes on pages 84–87 by Steven Wheeler

# CONTENTS

The Principles of Chinese Cooking      8

Appetizers      10

Soups      22

Seafood Dishes      30

Poultry Dishes      44

Pork Dishes      54

Beef and Lamb Dishes      62

Vegetable Dishes      66

Rice, Noodles and Dim Sum      74

Desserts      88

Stockists and Acknowledgements      92

Index      94

# TASTE OF CHINA

## DEH-TA HSIUNG

China is a vast country — about the same size as Western Europe or the United States — and its climate and food products are similarly varied. Consequently, each region has a very distinctive style of cooking, resulting in the world's most diverse cuisine.

Yet the fundamental character of Chinese cooking remains the same throughout the land. From Peking in the north to Canton in the south and Shanghai in the east to Sichuan in the west, different ingredients are all prepared, cooked and served in accordance with the same centuries-old principles.

# THE PRINCIPLES OF CHINESE COOKING

Chinese cooking is distinguished from all other food cultures in its emphasis on the harmonious blending of colour, aroma, flavour and texture both in a single dish and in a course of dishes for a meal.
Balance and contrast are the key words, based on the ancient Taoist philosophy of yin and yang. Consciously or unconsciously, any Chinese cook, from the housewife to the professional chef, will work to this yin-yang principle, and will vary ingredients, shapes, seasonings and cooking methods accordingly.
In order to achieve this, two important factors should be observed: the degree of heat and duration of cooking, which in turn means applying the right cooking method to the right food. The size and shape of a particular ingredient must be appropriate to the chosen method of cooking. Ingredients for quick stir-frying, for instance, should be cut into small, thin slices or shreds of uniform size, instead of large, thick chunks. This is not just for the sake of appearance, but because ingredients of the same size and shape will retain their natural colour, aroma and flavour and achieve the required texture if they are cooked for the same amount of time.

## EQUIPMENT AND UTENSILS

There are only a few basic implements essential to Chinese cooking and equivalent equipment is always available in a Western kitchen. However, authentic Chinese cooking utensils are of an ancient design, are usually made of inexpensive materials, and have been in continuous use for several thousand years. They do serve a special function, which is not always fulfilled by their more sophisticated and expensive Western counterparts.

**Chinese cleaver** (1) This is an all-purpose cook's knife used for slicing, shredding, peeling, crushing and chopping. Different sizes and weights are available.
**Ladle and spatula** (2) Some wok sets consist of a pair of stirrers in the form of a ladle and spatula. Of the two, the flat ladle or scooper (as it is sometimes called) is more versatile. It is used by Chinese cooks for adding ingredients and seasonings to the wok as well as for stirring.
**Sand-pot (casserole)** (3) Made of earthenware, casseroles are always used for braising and slow cooking on the stove top as they retain an even heat.
**Steamer** (4) The traditional Chinese steamer is made of bamboo, and the modern version is made of aluminium. The wok can also be used as a steamer with a rack or trivet and the dome-shaped wok lid.

**Strainer** (5) There are two basic types of strainer. One is made of copper or steel wire with a long bamboo handle, the other of perforated iron or stainless steel. Several different sizes are available.
**Wok** (6) The round-bottomed iron wok conducts and retains heat evenly. Because of its shape, the ingredients always return to the centre where the heat is most intense. The wok has many functions. It is ideal for deep-frying because its shape requires far less oil than the flat-bottomed deep-fryer. It also has more depth, which means more heat is generated, and a larger cooking surface, which means more food can be cooked at one time. Besides being a frying pan, the wok is also used for braising, steaming, boiling and poaching – in fact, the whole spectrum of Chinese cooking methods can be executed in one single utensil.

## INGREDIENTS

**Agar-agar** (1) Also known as isinglass (*Kanten* in Japanese), agar-agar is a product of seaweed and is sold dried in paper-thin strands or powdered form. Gelatine may be substituted.
**Baby corn cobs** (2) Baby corn cobs have a wonderfully sweet fragrance and flavour, and an irresistible texture. They are available both fresh and canned.
**Bamboo shoots** (3) Bamboo shoots are available in cans only. Once opened, the contents may be kept in fresh water in a covered jar for up to a week in the refrigerator. Try to get winter bamboo shoots, which have a firmer texture. Ready sliced bamboo shoots are also available.
**Bean curd (tofu)** (4) This custard-like preparation of puréed and pressed soya beans is exceptionally high in protein. It is usually sold in cakes about 7.5cm/3in square and 2.5cm/1in thick and can be found in Oriental and health food stores. It will keep for a few days if submerged in water in a container and placed in the refrigerator.
**Bean sprouts** (5) Fresh bean sprouts, from mung or soya beans, are widely available from Oriental stores and all supermarkets. They can be kept in the refrigerator for two to three days.
**Black bean sauce** (6) Black bean sauce is made up of salted black beans crushed and mixed with flour and spices (such as ginger, garlic or chilli) to make a thickish paste. Sold in jars or cans; once opened, it should be kept in the refrigerator.
**Chilli bean sauce** (7) Chilli bean sauce is made from fermented bean paste mixed with hot chilli and other seasonings. Sold in jars, some chilli bean sauces are quite mild, but some are very hot. You will have to try out the various brands yourself to see which one is to your taste.
**Chilli oil** (8) Chilli oil is made from dried red chillies, garlic, onions, salt and vegetable oil. It is used more as a dip than as a cooking ingredient.
**Chilli sauce** (9) This is a very hot sauce made from chillies, vinegar, sugar

and salt. Usually sold in bottles, it should be used sparingly in cooking or as a dip. Tabasco sauce can be a substitute.

**Chinese leaves** (10) There are two widely available varieties of Chinese leaves (also known as Chinese cabbage) found in supermarkets and greengrocers. The most commonly seen variety has a pale green colour and tightly-wrapped elongated head, and about two-thirds of the cabbage is stem which has a crunchy texture. The other variety found has a shorter and fatter head with curlier, pale yellow or green leaves, and white stems.

**Coriander** (11) Fresh coriander leaves, also known as Chinese parsley or *cilantro*, are widely used in Chinese cooking as a garnish.

**Dried Chinese mushrooms** (shiitake) (12) These highly fragrant dried mushrooms are sold in plastic bags. They are not cheap, but a small amount will go a long way, and they will keep indefinitely in an airtight jar. Soak them in warm water for 20–30 minutes (or in cold water for several hours), squeeze dry and discard the hard stalks before use.

**Egg noodles** (13) There are many varieties of noodles in China – ranging from flat, broad ribbons to long and narrow strands. Both dried and fresh noodles are available.

**Five-spice powder** (14) A mixture of star anise, fennel seeds, cloves, cinnamon bark and Sichuan pepper make up five-spice powder. It is highly piquant, so should be used very sparingly, and will keep indefinitely in an airtight container.

**Ginger root** (15) Fresh ginger, sold by weight, should be peeled and sliced and finely chopped or shredded before use. It will keep for weeks in a dry, cool place. Dried ginger powder is no substitute.

**Hoi Sin sauce** (16) This tasty sauce is also known as barbecue sauce, and is made from soy beans, sugar, flour, vinegar, salt, garlic, chilli and sesame seed oil. Sold in cans or jars, it will keep in the refrigerator for several months.

**Oyster sauce** (17) This soya based, thickish sauce is used as a flavouring in Cantonese cooking. Sold in bottles, it will keep in the refrigerator for months.

**Plum sauce** (18) Plum sauce has a unique fruity flavour – a sweet and sour sauce with a difference.

**Red bean paste** (19) This reddish-brown paste is made from puréed red beans and crystallized sugar. Sold in cans, the left-over contents should be transferred to a covered container and will keep in the refrigerator for several months.

**Rice vinegar** (20) There are two basic types of rice vinegar – red vinegar is made from fermented rice and has a distinctive dark colour and depth of flavour; white vinegar is stronger in flavour as it is distilled from rice.

**Rice wine** (21) Chinese rice wine, made from glutinous rice, is also known as 'Yellow wine' (*Huang Jiu* or *Chiew* in Chinese), because of its golden amber colour. The best variety is called Shao Hsing or Shaoxing from the southeast of China. A good dry or medium sherry can be an acceptable substitute.

**Rock sugar** (22) Rock sugar is made with a combination of cane sugar and honey. It adds a special sheen to foods that have been stewed with it.

**Salted black beans** (23) Salted black beans are very salty and pungent. They are sold in plastic bags, jars or cans and should be crushed with water or wine before use. The beans will keep almost indefinitely in a covered jar.

**Sesame oil** (24) Sesame oil is sold in bottles and widely used in China as a garnish rather than for cooking. The refined yellow sesame oil sold in Middle Eastern stores is not so aromatic .

a very satisfactory substitute

**Sichuan peppercorns** (25) Also known as *farchiew*, these are wild red peppers from Sichuan. More aromatic but less hot than either white or black peppers, they do give quite a unique flavour to the food.

**Soy sauce** (26) Sold in bottles or cans, this most popular Chinese sauce is used both for cooking and at the table. Light soy sauce has more flavour than the sweeter dark soy sauce, which gives the food a rich, reddish colour.

**Straw mushrooms** (*Volvariella volvacea*) (27) Grown on beds of rice straw, hence the name, straw mushrooms have a pleasant slippery texture and a subtle taste. Canned straw mushrooms should be rinsed and drained.

**Water chestnuts** (28) Water chestnuts are not nuts as they are the roots of a plant (*Heleocharis tuberosa*). They are also known as horse's hooves in China,

on account of their appearance before the skin is peeled off and are available fresh or in cans. Canned water chestnuts retain only part of the texture, and even less of the flavour, of fresh ones. They will keep for about a month in the refrigerator in a covered jar, if the water is changed every two days.

**Wonton skins** (29) Made from wheat flour, egg and water, these wafer-thin wonton wrappers are sold in 7.5cm/3in squares from Oriental stores. They can be frozen, and will keep for up to six months.

**Wood-ears** (30) Also known as cloud-ears, these are dried black fungus (*Auricularia polytricha*). Sold in plastic bags in Oriental stores, wood-ears should be soaked in cold or warm water for 20 minutes, then rinsed in fresh water before use. They have a crunchy texture and a mild but subtle flavour.

**Yellow bean sauce** (31) Yellow bean sauce is a thick paste made from salted, fermented yellow soya beans, crushed with flour and sugar. It will keep in the refrigerator for months if stored in a screw-top jar.

# CRISPY SPRING ROLLS

*Zha Chu Kuen*

These small and dainty vegetarian spring rolls are ideal served as appetizers, or as cocktail snacks. For a non-vegetarian version, just replace the mushrooms with chicken or pork, and the carrots with shrimp.

**MAKES 40 ROLLS**

**Ingredients**
225g/8oz fresh bean sprouts
115g/4oz tender leeks or spring onions (scallions)
115g/4oz carrots
115g/4oz bamboo shoots, sliced
115g/4oz white mushrooms
3–4 tbsp vegetable oil
1 tsp salt
1 tsp light brown sugar
1 tbsp light soy sauce

1 tbsp Chinese rice wine or dry sherry
20 frozen spring roll skins, defrosted
1 tbsp cornflour (cornstarch) paste
flour, for dusting
oil, for deep-frying

### Cornflour (cornstarch) paste

To make cornflour (cornstarch) paste, mix 4 parts dry cornflour (cornstarch) with about 5 parts cold water until smooth.

1 Cut all the vegetables into thin shreds, roughly the same size and shape as the bean sprouts.

2 Heat the oil in a wok and stir-fry the vegetables for about 1 minute. Add the salt, sugar, soy sauce and wine or sherry and continue stirring for 1½–2 minutes. Remove and drain the excess liquid, then leave to cool.

3 To make the spring rolls, cut each spring roll skin in half diagonally, then place about 1 tbsp of the vegetable mixture one-third of the way down on the skin, with the triangle pointing away from you.

4 Lift the lower flap over the filling and roll once.

5 Fold in both ends and roll once more, then brush the upper edge with a little cornflour (cornstarch) paste, and roll into a neat package. Lightly dust a tray with flour and place the spring rolls on the tray with the flap-side down.

6 To cook, heat the oil in a wok or deep-fryer until hot, then reduce the heat to low. Deep-fry the spring rolls in batches (about 8–10 at a time) for 2–3 minutes or until golden and crispy, then remove and drain. Serve the spring rolls hot with a dip sauce such as soy sauce or Spicy Salt and Pepper.

# DEEP-FRIED SPARERIBS WITH SPICY SALT AND PEPPER

*Zha Pai Ku*

Ideally, each sparerib should be chopped into 3–4 bite-sized pieces before or after cooking. If this is not possible, then serve the ribs whole.

### SERVES 4–6

**Ingredients**
10–12 finger ribs, weighing in total about 675g/
    1½lb, with excess fat and gristle trimmed
about 2–3 tbsp flour
vegetable oil, for deep-frying

**Marinade**
1 clove garlic, crushed and finely chopped
1 tbsp light brown sugar
1 tbsp light soy sauce
1 tbsp dark soy sauce
2 tbsp Chinese rice wine or dry sherry
½ tsp chilli sauce
few drops sesame oil

### Spicy Salt and Pepper

To make Spicy Salt and Pepper, mix 1 tbsp salt with 2 tsp ground Sichuan peppercorns and 1 tsp five-spice powder. Heat together in a preheated dry pan for about 2 minutes over low heat, stirring constantly. This quantity is sufficient for at least six servings.

1 Chop each rib into 3–4 pieces, then mix with all the marinade ingredients, and marinate for at least 2–3 hours .

2 Coat the ribs with flour and deep-fry in medium-hot oil for 4–5 minutes, stirring to separate. Remove and drain.

3 Heat the oil to high and deep-fry the ribs once more for about 1 minute, or until the colour is an even dark brown. Remove and drain, then serve with Spicy Salt and Pepper.

# DEEP-FRIED SQUID WITH SPICY SALT AND PEPPER

*Jiao Yan You Yu*

This recipe is from the Cantonese school of cuisine, where seafood is one of their specialities.

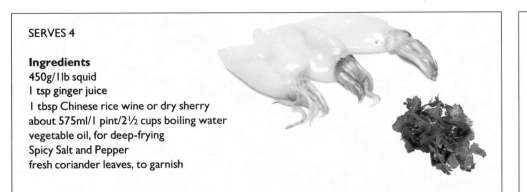

**SERVES 4**

**Ingredients**
450g/1lb squid
1 tsp ginger juice
1 tbsp Chinese rice wine or dry sherry
about 575ml/1 pint/2½ cups boiling water
vegetable oil, for deep-frying
Spicy Salt and Pepper
fresh coriander leaves, to garnish

### Ginger juice

To make ginger juice, mix finely-chopped or grated fresh ginger with an equal quantity of cold water and place in damp muslin (cheesecloth). Twist tightly to extract the juice. Alternatively, crush the ginger in a garlic press.

1 Clean the squid by discarding the head and the transparent backbone as well as the ink bag; peel off and discard the thin skin, then wash the squid and dry well. Open up the squid and, using a sharp knife, score the inside of the flesh in a criss-cross pattern.

2 Cut the squid into pieces each about the size of an oblong postage stamp. Marinate in a bowl with the ginger juice and wine or sherry for 25–30 minutes.

3 Blanch the squid in boiling water for a few seconds – each piece will curl up and the criss-cross pattern will open out to resemble ears of corn. Remove and drain. Dry well.

4 Deep-fry the squid in hot oil for 15–20 seconds only, remove quickly and drain. Sprinkle with the Spicy Salt and Pepper and serve garnished with fresh coriander leaves.

# BON-BON CHICKEN WITH SESAME SAUCE

### *Bon Bon Ji*

The chicken meat is tenderized by being beaten with a stick (called a *bon* in Chinese), hence the name for this very popular Sichuan dish.

**SERVES 6–8**

**Ingredients**
1 whole chicken weighing about 1kg/2¼lb
1.1 litre/2 pints/5 cups water
1 tbsp sesame oil
shredded cucumber, to garnish

**Sauce**
2 tbsp light soy sauce
1 tsp sugar

1 tbsp finely-chopped spring onions (scallions)
1 tsp red chilli oil
½ tsp ground Sichuan peppercorns
1 tsp white sesame seeds
2 tbsp sesame paste, or 2 tbsp peanut butter
    creamed with a little sesame oil

1 Clean the chicken well. In a wok or saucepan bring the water to a rolling boil, add the chicken, reduce the heat and cook under cover for 40–45 minutes. Remove the chicken and immerse in cold water to cool.

2 After at least 1 hour, remove the chicken and drain; dry well with kitchen paper and brush on a coating of sesame oil. Carve the meat off the legs, wings and breast and pull the meat off the rest of the bones.

3 On a flat surface, pound the meat with a rolling pin, then tear the meat into shreds with your fingers.

4 Place the meat in a dish with the shredded cucumber around the edge. In a bowl, mix together all the sauce ingredients, keeping a few spring onions (scallions) to garnish. Pour over the chicken and serve.

# DEEP-FRIED WONTON SKINS WITH SWEET AND SOUR SAUCE

*Cha Won Tun*

Ready-made fresh or frozen wonton skins are available from Oriental stores.

SERVES 4–6

**Ingredients**
16–20 ready-made wonton skins
vegetable oil, for deep-frying

**Sauce**
1 tbsp vegetable oil
2 tbsp light brown sugar
3 tbsp rice vinegar
1 tbsp light soy sauce
1 tbsp tomato sauce (ketchup)
3–4 tbsp Basic Stock or water
1 tbsp cornflour (cornstarch) paste

1 Pinch the centre of each wonton skin and twist it around to form a floral shape.

2 Deep-fry the floral wonton skins in hot oil for 1–2 minutes, or until crispy. Remove and drain.

3 Heat the oil in a wok or saucepan, add the sugar, vinegar, soy sauce, tomato sauce (ketchup) and stock or water.

4 Thicken the sauce with the cornflour (cornstarch) paste, stirring until smooth, and pour it over the wonton skins. Serve immediately.

# CRISPY 'SEAWEED'

## *Cai Sung*

Surprisingly, the very popular 'seaweed' served in Chinese restaurants is, in fact, ordinary spring greens (collard)!

| SERVES 4–6 | vegetable oil, for deep-frying |
| --- | --- |
| | ½ tsp salt |
| **Ingredients** | I tsp caster (superfine) sugar |
| 450g/1lb spring greens (collard) | I tbsp ground fried fish, to garnish (optional) |

1 Cut off the hard stalks in the centre of each spring green (collard) leaf. Pile the leaves on top of each other, and roll into a tight 'sausage'. Thinly cut the leaves into fine shreds. Spread them out to dry.

2 Heat the oil in a wok or deep-fryer until hot. Deep-fry the shredded greens in batches, stirring to separate them.

3 Remove the greens with a slotted spoon as soon as they are crispy, but before they turn brown. Drain. Sprinkle the salt and sugar evenly all over the 'seaweed'; mix well, garnish with ground fish and serve.

---

# SESAME SEED PRAWN (SHRIMP) TOASTS

## *Hsia Jen Tu Ssu*

Use uncooked prawns (shrimp) for this dish, as ready-cooked ones will separate from the bread during cooking.

| SERVES 6–8 | salt and pepper, to taste | I tbsp cornflour (cornstarch) paste |
| --- | --- | --- |
| | I egg white, lightly beaten | 115–140g/4–5oz/1 cup white sesame seeds |
| **Ingredients** | I tsp finely-chopped spring onions (scallions) | 6 large slices white bread |
| 225g/8oz prawns (shrimp), peeled | ½ tsp finely-chopped fresh ginger | vegetable oil, for deep-frying |
| 25g/1oz/¼ stick lard (shortening) | I tbsp Chinese rice wine or dry sherry | |

1 Chop together the prawns with the lard (shortening) to form a smooth paste. In a bowl, mix with all the other ingredients except the sesame seeds and bread.

2 Spread the sesame seeds evenly on a large plate or tray; spread the prawn paste thickly on one side of each slice of bread, then press, spread-side down, onto the seeds.

3 Heat the oil in a wok until medium-hot; fry 2–3 slices at a time, spread-side down, for 2–3 minutes. Remove and drain. Cut into 6–8 fingers (without crusts).

# PICKLED SWEET AND SOUR CUCUMBER

## *Tan Chu Huang Gua*

The 'pickling' can be done in hours rather than days – but the more time you have, the better the result.

| SERVES 6–8 | 2 tsp caster (superfine) sugar |
|---|---|
| | 1 tsp rice vinegar |
| **Ingredients** | ½ tsp red chilli oil (optional) |
| 1 slender cucumber, about 30cm/12in long | few drops sesame oil |
| 1 tsp salt | |

1 Halve the unpeeled cucumber lengthways. Scrape out the seeds and cut across the cucumber into thick chunks.

2 In a bowl, sprinkle the cucumber chunks with the salt and mix well. Leave for at least 20–30 minutes – longer if possible – then pour the juice away.

3 Mix the cucumber with the sugar, vinegar and chilli oil, if using. Sprinkle with the sesame oil just before serving.

# HOT AND SOUR CABBAGE

## *Suan La Pai Cai*

Another popular recipe from Sichuan – this dish can be served hot or cold.

| SERVES 6–8 | 3–4 tbsp vegetable oil | 1 tbsp light brown sugar |
|---|---|---|
| | 10–12 red Sichuan peppercorns | 1 tbsp light soy sauce |
| **Ingredients** | few whole dried red chillies | 2 tbsp rice vinegar |
| 450g/1lb pale green or white cabbage | 1 tsp salt | few drops sesame oil |

1 Cut the cabbage leaves into small pieces each roughly 2.5 × 1.25cm (1 × ½ in).

2 Heat the oil in a preheated wok until smoking, then add the peppercorns and chillies.

3 Add the cabbage to the wok and stir-fry for about 1–2 minutes. Add the salt and sugar, continue stirring for another minute, then add the soy sauce, vinegar and sesame oil. Blend well and serve.

# BUTTERFLY PRAWNS (SHRIMP)

*Feng Wei Xia*

For best results, use uncooked giant or king prawns (shrimp) in their shells. Sold headless, they are about 8–10cm/3–4in long, and you should get 18–20 prawns (shrimp) per 450g/1lb.

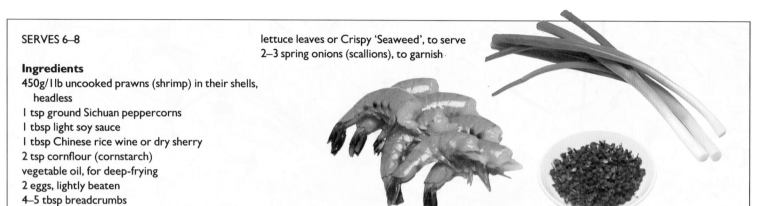

**SERVES 6–8**

**Ingredients**
450g/1lb uncooked prawns (shrimp) in their shells, headless
1 tsp ground Sichuan peppercorns
1 tbsp light soy sauce
1 tbsp Chinese rice wine or dry sherry
2 tsp cornflour (cornstarch)
vegetable oil, for deep-frying
2 eggs, lightly beaten
4–5 tbsp breadcrumbs

lettuce leaves or Crispy 'Seaweed', to serve
2–3 spring onions (scallions), to garnish

1 Peel the prawns (shrimp) but leave the tails on. Split the prawns (shrimp) in half from the underbelly, about three-quarters of the way through, leaving the tails still firmly attached.

2 In a bowl, marinate with the pepper, soy sauce, wine or sherry and cornflour (cornstarch) for 10–15 minutes.

3 Heat the oil in a wok or deep-fryer until medium-hot. Pick up one prawn (shrimp) at a time by the tail, and dip it in the egg.

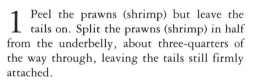

4 Roll the egg-covered prawns (shrimp) in breadcrumbs.

5 Heat the oil in the wok until medium-hot. Gently lower the prawns (shrimp) into the oil.

6 Deep-fry the prawns (shrimp) in batches until golden brown. Remove and drain. To serve, arrange the prawns (shrimp) neatly on a bed of lettuce leaves or Crispy 'Seaweed', and garnish with spring onions (scallions), which are either raw or have been soaked for about 30 seconds in hot oil.

# BASIC STOCK

## *Qing Tang*

The basic stock is used not only as the basis for soup making, but also for general use in cooking whenever liquid is required instead of plain water.

**MAKES 2.25L/4 PINTS/10½ CUPS**

**Ingredients**
675g/1½lb chicken pieces
675g/1½lb pork spareribs
3.25 litres/6 pints/15 cups cold water
3–4 pieces fresh ginger, unpeeled and crushed
3–4 spring onions (scallions), each tied into a knot
3–4 tbsp Chinese rice wine or dry sherry

1 Trim off any excess fat from the chicken and spareribs and chop them into large pieces.

2 Place the chicken and spareribs into a large pot or pan with the water. Add the ginger and spring onion (scallion) knots.

3 Bring to the boil and, using a sieve (strainer), skim off the froth. Reduce the heat and simmer, uncovered, for 2–3 hours.

4 Strain the stock, discarding the chicken, pork, ginger and spring onions (scallions); add the wine or sherry and return to the boil. Simmer for 2–3 minutes. Refrigerate the stock when cool. It will keep for up to 4–5 days. Alternatively, it can be frozen in small containers and defrosted when required.

# HOT AND SOUR SOUP

*Suan La Tang*

This surely must be the all-time favourite soup in Chinese restaurants and take-aways throughout the world. It is fairly simple to make once you have got all the necessary ingredients together.

**SERVES 4**

**Ingredients**
4–6 dried Chinese mushrooms (shiitake), soaked
115g/4oz pork or chicken
I cake bean curd (tofu)
50g/2oz sliced bamboo shoots, drained

575ml/I pint/2½ cups Basic Stock
I tbsp Chinese rice wine or dry sherry
I tbsp light soy sauce
I tbsp rice vinegar
salt, to taste
½ tsp ground white pepper
I tbsp cornflour (cornstarch) paste

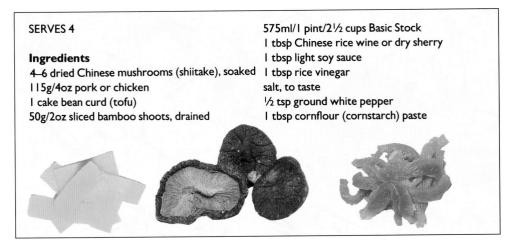

1 Squeeze the soaked mushrooms dry, then discard the hard stalks. Thinly shred the mushrooms, meat, bean curd (tofu) and bamboo shoots.

2 In a wok or saucepan, bring the stock to a rolling boil and add the shredded ingredients. Bring back to the boil and simmer for about 1 minute.

3 Add the seasonings and bring back to the boil once more. Now add the cornflour (cornstarch) paste and stir until thickened. Serve hot.

# CORN AND CRABMEAT/CHICKEN SOUP

*Xie Rou Yumi Tang*

This soup originated in the USA but it has since been introduced into China. You must use creamed corn in the recipe to achieve the right consistency.

**SERVES 4**

**Ingredients**
115g/4oz crabmeat or chicken breast fillet
½ tsp finely-chopped fresh ginger
2 egg whites
2 tbsp milk

1 tbsp cornflour (cornstarch) paste
575ml/1 pint/2½ cups Basic Stock
225g/8oz can creamed corn
salt and pepper, to taste
finely-chopped spring onions (scallions), to garnish

1 Flake the crabmeat (or coarsely chop the chicken breast) and mix with the ginger.

2 Beat the egg whites until frothy, add the milk and cornflour (cornstarch) paste and beat again until smooth. Blend with the crabmeat or chicken breast.

3 In a wok or saucepan, bring the stock to the boil, add the creamed sweetcorn and bring back to the boil once more.

4 Stir in the crabmeat or chicken breast and egg-white mixture, adjust the seasonings and stir gently until well blended. Serve garnished with finely-chopped spring onions (scallions).

# CHICKEN AND ASPARAGUS SOUP

*Lusun Ji Rou Tang*

This is a very delicate and delicious soup. When fresh asparagus is not in season, canned white asparagus is an acceptable substitute.

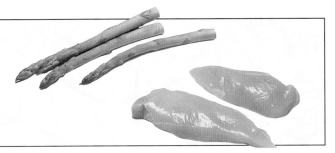

SERVES 4

**Ingredients**
140g/5oz chicken breast fillet
pinch of salt
1 tsp egg white
1 tsp cornflour (cornstarch) paste

115g/4oz asparagus
700ml/1 ¼ pints/3 cups Basic Stock
salt and pepper, to taste
fresh coriander leaves, to garnish

1 Cut the chicken meat into thin slices each about the size of a postage stamp. Mix with a pinch of salt, then add the egg white, and finally the cornflour (cornstarch) paste.

2 Discard the tough stems of the asparagus, and diagonally cut the tender spears into short lengths.

3 In a wok or saucepan, bring the stock to a rolling boil, add the asparagus and bring back to the boil, cooking for 2 minutes. (This is not necessary if using canned asparagus.)

4 Add the chicken, stir to separate and bring back to the boil once more. Adjust the seasonings. Serve hot, garnished with fresh coriander leaves.

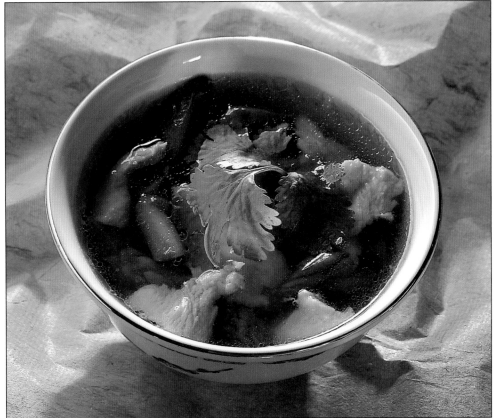

# SPINACH AND BEAN CURD (TOFU) SOUP

*Pao Cai Dao Fu Tang*

This soup is delicious. If fresh spinach is not in season, watercress or lettuce can be used instead.

| SERVES 4 | 115g/4oz spinach leaves (weight exclusive of stems) | salt and pepper, to taste |
| --- | --- | --- |
| **Ingredients** | 700ml/1 ¼ pints/3 cups Basic Stock |  |
| 1 cake bean curd (tofu) | 1 tbsp light soy sauce | |

1 Cut the bean curd (tofu) into 12 small pieces, each about 0.5cm/¼in thick. Wash the spinach leaves and cut them into small pieces.

2 In a wok or saucepan, bring the stock to a rolling boil. Add the bean curd (tofu) and soy sauce, bring back to the boil and simmer for about 2 minutes.

3 Add the spinach and simmer for a further minute. Skim the surface to make it clear, then adjust the seasoning and serve.

# SLICED FISH AND CORIANDER SOUP

*Yu Pian Yen Hsee Tang*

It is not necessary to remove the skin from the fish, as it helps to keep the flesh together when cooked.

| SERVES 4 | 1 tsp egg white | salt and pepper, to taste |
| --- | --- | --- |
| | 2 tsp cornflour (cornstarch) paste |  |
| **Ingredients** | 700ml/1 ¼ pints/3 cups Basic Stock | |
| 225g/8oz white fish fillet such as lemon sole or plaice | 1 tbsp light soy sauce | |
| | about 50g/2oz fresh coriander leaves, chopped | |

1 Cut the fish into large slices each about the size of a matchbox. Mix with the egg white and cornflour (cornstarch) paste.

2 In a wok or saucepan, bring the stock to a rolling boil and poach the fish slices for about 1 minute.

3 Add the soy sauce and coriander leaves, adjust the seasonings and serve.

# THREE-DELICACY SOUP

*San Xian Tang*

This delicious soup combines the three ingredients of chicken, ham and prawns (shrimp).

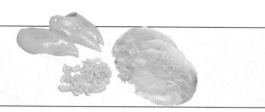

| SERVES 4 | 115g/4oz honey-roast ham |
|---|---|
| | 115g/4oz peeled prawns (shrimp) |
| **Ingredients** | 700ml/1¼ pints/3 cups Basic Stock |
| 115g/4oz chicken breast fillet | salt, to taste |

### Cook's tip

Fresh, uncooked prawns impart the best flavour. If these are not available you can use ready-cooked prawns. They must be added at the last stage to prevent over-cooking.

1 Thinly slice the chicken and ham into small pieces. If the prawns (shrimp) are large, cut each in half lengthways.

2 In a wok or saucepan, bring the stock to a rolling boil, add the chicken, ham and prawns (shrimp). Bring back to the boil, add the salt and simmer for 1 minute. Serve hot.

# LAMB AND CUCUMBER SOUP

*Yang Rou Huang Gua Tang*

This is a variation on Hot and Sour Soup, but is much simpler to prepare.

| SERVES 4 | 1 tbsp light soy sauce | 700ml/1¼ pints/3 cups Basic Stock |
|---|---|---|
| | 2 tsp Chinese rice wine or dry sherry | 1 tbsp rice vinegar |
| **Ingredients** | ½ tsp sesame oil | salt and ground white pepper, to taste |
| 225g/8oz lamb steak | 1 piece cucumber, 7.5cm/3in long | |

1 Trim off any excess fat from the lamb and discard. Thinly slice the lamb into small pieces. Marinate with the soy sauce, wine or sherry and sesame oil for 25–30 minutes. Discard the marinade.

2 Halve the cucumber piece lengthways (do not peel), then cut into thin slices diagonally.

3 In a wok or saucepan, bring the stock to a rolling boil, add the lamb and stir to separate. Return to the boil, then add the cucumber slices, vinegar and seasonings. Bring to the boil once more, and serve at once.

# FRIED SEAFOOD WITH VEGETABLES

*Chao San Xian*

Another colourful and delicious dish from south-east China, combining prawns (shrimp), squid and scallops. The squid can be replaced by another fish, or omitted altogether.

**SERVES 4**

**Ingredients**
115g/4oz squid, cleaned
4–6 fresh scallops
115g/4oz uncooked prawns (shrimp)
½ egg white
1 tbsp cornflour (cornstarch) paste
2–3 stalks of celery
1 small red (bell) pepper, cored and seeded
2 small carrots
about 300ml/½ pint/1¼ cups oil

½ tsp finely-chopped fresh ginger
1 spring onion (scallion), cut into short sections
1 tsp salt
½ tsp light brown sugar
1 tbsp Chinese rice wine or dry sherry
1 tbsp light soy sauce
1 tsp chilli bean sauce
2 tbsp Basic Stock
few drops sesame oil

1 Open up the squid and, using a sharp knife, score the inside in a criss-cross pattern. Cut the squid into pieces each about the size of an oblong stamp. Soak the squid in a bowl of boiling water until all the pieces curl up; rinse in cold water and drain.

2 Cut each scallop into 3–4 slices. Peel the prawns (shrimp) and cut each in half lengthways. Mix the scallops and prawns (shrimp) with the egg white and cornflour (cornstarch) paste.

3 Cut the celery, red (bell) pepper and carrots into thin slices, each about the size of a postage stamp.

4 Heat the oil in a preheated wok until medium-hot and stir-fry the seafood for about 30–40 seconds. Remove with a strainer and drain.

5 Pour off the excess oil, leaving about 2 tbsp in the wok, and add the vegetables with the ginger and spring onions (scallions). Stir-fry for about 1 minute.

6 Add the seafood to the wok, stir for another 30–40 seconds, then add the salt, sugar, wine or sherry, soy sauce and chilli bean sauce. Blend well, add the stock and continue stirring for another minute. Then serve garnished with sesame oil.

# BRAISED FISH FILLET WITH MUSHROOMS

*Chin Chao Yu Tiao*

This is the Chinese version of the French *filets de sole bonne femme* (sole with mushrooms and wine sauce).

| SERVES 4 | 2 tbsp cornflour (cornstarch) paste | 1 tbsp light soy sauce |
| --- | --- | --- |
| **Ingredients** | about 575ml/1 pint/2½ cups vegetable oil | 2 tbsp Chinese rice wine or dry sherry |
| 450g/1 lb fillet of lemon sole or plaice | 1 tbsp finely-chopped spring onions (scallions) | 1 tbsp brandy |
| 1 tsp salt | ½ tsp finely-chopped fresh ginger | about 100ml/4fl oz/½ cup Basic Stock |
| ½ egg white | 115g/4oz white mushrooms, thinly sliced | few drops sesame oil, to garnish |
| | 1 tsp light brown sugar | |

1 Trim off the soft bones along the edge of the fish, but leave the skin on. Cut each fillet into bite-sized pieces. Mix the fish with a little salt, the egg white and about half of the cornflour (cornstarch) paste.

2 Heat the oil until medium-hot, add the fish slice by slice and stir gently so the pieces do not stick. Remove after about 1 minute and drain. Pour off the excess oil, leaving about 2 tbsp in the wok.

3 Stir-fry the onions (scallions), ginger and mushrooms for 1 minute. Add the other ingredients except the cornflour (cornstarch) paste. Bring to the boil. Braise the fish for 1 minute. Thicken with the paste, and garnish.

# PRAWN (SHRIMP) FU-YUNG

*Fu Ron Xia*

This is a very colourful dish that is simple to make. Most of the preparation can be done well in advance.

| SERVES 4 | 1 tsp salt | 3–4 tbsp vegetable oil |
| --- | --- | --- |
| | 225g/8oz uncooked prawns (shrimp), peeled | 175g/6oz green peas |
| **Ingredients** | 2 tsp cornflour (cornstarch) paste | 1 tbsp Chinese rice wine or dry sherry |
| 3 eggs, beaten, reserving 1 tsp of egg white | 1 tbsp finely-chopped spring onions (scallions) | |

1 Beat the eggs with a pinch of the salt and a few bits of the spring onions (scallions). In a wok, scramble the eggs in a little oil over moderate heat. Remove and reserve.

2 Mix the prawns (shrimp) with a little salt, 1 tsp of egg white, and the cornflour (cornstarch) paste. Stir-fry the peas in hot oil for 30 seconds. Add the prawns (shrimp).

3 Add the spring onions (scallions). Stir-fry for another minute. Then stir the mixture into the scrambled egg with a little salt and the wine or sherry. Blend well and serve.

# Sweet and Sour Prawns (Shrimp)

## *Tang Cu Xia*

It is best to use uncooked prawns (shrimp) if available. If using ready-cooked ones, they can be added to the sauce without the initial deep frying.

SERVES 4–6

**Ingredients**
450g/1lb king prawns (shrimp) in their shells
vegetable oil, for deep-frying
lettuce leaves, to serve

**Sauce**
1 tbsp vegetable oil

1 tbsp finely-chopped spring onions (scallions)
2 tsp finely-chopped fresh ginger
2 tbsp light soy sauce
2 tbsp light brown sugar
3 tbsp rice vinegar
1 tbsp Chinese rice wine or dry sherry
about 100ml/4fl oz/½ cup Basic Stock
1 tbsp cornflour (cornstarch) paste
few drops sesame oil

1 Pull the soft legs off the prawns (shrimp) without removing the shells. Dry well with kitchen paper.

2 Deep-fry the prawns (shrimp) in hot oil for 35–40 seconds, or until their colour changes from grey to bright orange. Remove and drain.

3 To make the sauce, heat the oil in a preheated wok, add the spring onions (scallions) and ginger, followed by the seasonings and stock, and bring to the boil.

4 Add the prawns (shrimp) to the sauce, blend well, then thicken the sauce with the cornflour (cornstarch) paste, stirring until smooth. Sprinkle with the sesame oil. Serve on a bed of lettuce leaves.

# STIR-FRIED PRAWNS (SHRIMP) WITH BROCCOLI

*Xi Lan Chao Xia Ren*

This is a very colourful dish, highly nutritious and at the same time extremely delicious; furthermore, it is not time-consuming or difficult to prepare.

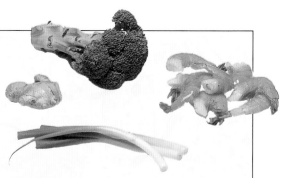

SERVES 4

**Ingredients**
175–225g/6–8oz prawns (shrimp), shelled and deveined
1 tsp salt
1 tbsp Chinese rice wine or dry sherry
1 tbsp cornflour (cornstarch) paste
½ egg white

225g/8oz broccoli
about 300ml/½ pint/1¼ cups vegetable oil
1 spring onion (scallion), cut into short sections
1 tsp light brown sugar
about 2 tbsp Basic Stock or water
1 tsp light soy sauce
few drops sesame oil

1 Cut each prawn (shrimp) in half lengthways. Mix with a pinch of salt, and about 1 tsp of the wine, egg white and cornflour (cornstarch) paste.

2 Cut the broccoli heads into florets; remove the rough skin from the stalks, then diagonally slice the florets into diamond-shaped chunks.

3 Heat the oil in a preheated wok and stir-fry the prawns (shrimp) for about 30 seconds. Remove with a strainer and drain.

4 Pour off the excess oil, leaving 2 tbsp in the wok. Add the broccoli and spring onion (scallion), stir-fry for about 2 minutes, then add the remaining salt, and the sugar, followed by the prawns (shrimp) and stock or water. Add the soy sauce and remaining wine or sherry. Blend well, then finally add the sesame oil and serve.

# SQUID WITH GREEN (BELL) PEPPER AND BLACK BEAN SAUCE

*Si Jiao You Yu*

This dish is a product of the Cantonese school, and makes an attractive meal that is as delicious as it looks.

**SERVES 4**

**Ingredients**
350–400g/12–14oz squid
1 medium green (bell) pepper, cored and seeded
3–4 tbsp vegetable oil
1 clove garlic, finely chopped
½ tsp finely-chopped fresh ginger
1 tbsp finely-chopped spring onions (scallions)

1 tsp salt
1 tbsp black bean sauce
1 tbsp Chinese rice wine or dry sherry
few drops sesame oil

1 To clean the squid, discard the head, the transparent backbone and the ink bag. Peel off and discard the skin, then wash the squid and dry well. Open up the squid and, with a sharp knife, score the inside of the flesh in a criss-cross pattern.

2 Cut the squid into pieces each about the size of an oblong postage stamp. Blanch the squid in a pan of boiling water for a few seconds. Remove and drain; dry well.

3 Cut the green (bell) pepper into small triangular pieces. Heat the oil in a wok and stir-fry the green (bell) pepper for about 1 minute.

4 Add the garlic, ginger, spring onion (scallion), salt and squid, then continue stirring for another minute. Finally add the black bean sauce and wine or sherry, and blend well. Sprinkle with sesame oil and serve.

# FISH WITH SWEET AND SOUR SAUCE

*Wu Liu Yu*

Another name for this dish is Five-Willow Fish, after the five shredded ingredients in the dressing.

**SERVES 4–6**

**Ingredients**
1 carp, bream, sea bass, trout, grouper or grey
   mullet, weighing about 675g/1½lb, gutted
1 tsp salt
about 2 tbsp plain (all-purpose) flour
vegetable oil, for deep-frying
fresh coriander leaves, to garnish

**Sauce**
1 tbsp vegetable oil

50g/2oz carrot, thinly shredded
50g/2oz sliced bamboo shoots, drained and
   shredded
25g/1oz green (bell) pepper, thinly shredded
25g/1oz red (bell) pepper, thinly shredded
2–3 spring onions (scallions), finely shredded
1 tbsp thinly-shredded fresh ginger
1 tbsp light soy sauce
2 tbsp light brown sugar
2–3 tbsp rice vinegar
about 100ml/4fl oz/½ cup Basic Stock
1 tbsp cornflour (cornstarch) paste

1 Clean and dry the fish well. Using a sharp knife, score both sides of the fish as far in as the bone with diagonal cuts at intervals of about 2.5cm/1in.

2 Rub the whole fish with salt both inside and out, then coat it from head to tail with flour.

3 Deep-fry the fish in the hot oil for about 3–4 minutes on both sides, or until golden brown. Remove the fish and drain, then place on a heated platter.

4 For the sauce, heat the oil and stir-fry all the vegetables for about 1 minute, then add the seasoning. Blend well, add the stock and bring to the boil. Add the cornflour (cornstarch) paste, stirring well until the sauce thickens and is smooth. Pour the sauce over the fish and garnish with fresh coriander leaves.

# BRAISED WHOLE FISH IN CHILLI AND GARLIC SAUCE

*Gan Shao Yu*

This is a classic Sichuan recipe. When served in a restaurant, the fish's head and tail are usually discarded before cooking, and used in other dishes. A whole fish may be used, however, and always looks impressive, especially for formal occasions and dinner parties.

**SERVES 4–6**

**Ingredients**

1 carp, bream, sea bass, trout, grouper or grey
    mullet, weighing about 675g/1½lb, gutted
1 tbsp light soy sauce
1 tbsp Chinese rice wine or dry sherry
vegetable oil, for deep-frying

**Sauce**

2 cloves garlic, finely chopped
2–3 spring onions (scallions), finely chopped with
    the white and green parts separated

1 tsp finely-chopped fresh ginger
2 tbsp chilli bean sauce
1 tbsp tomato purée (paste)
2 tsp light brown sugar
1 tbsp rice vinegar
about 100ml/4fl oz/½ cup Basic Stock
1 tbsp cornflour (cornstarch) paste
few drops sesame oil

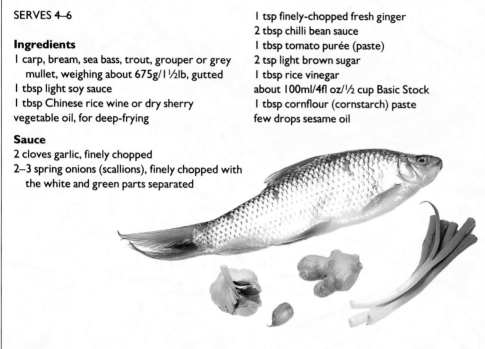

1  Rinse and dry the fish well. Using a sharp knife, score both sides of the fish as far down as the bone with diagonal cuts about 2.5cm/1in apart. Rub the whole fish with soy sauce and wine or sherry on both sides, then leave to marinate for 10–15 minutes.

2  In a wok, deep-fry the fish in hot oil for about 3–4 minutes on both sides or until golden brown.

3  Pour off the excess oil, leaving about 1 tbsp in the wok. Push the fish to one side of the wok and add the garlic, the white part of the spring onions (scallions), ginger, chilli bean sauce, tomato purée (paste), sugar, vinegar and stock. Bring to the boil and braise the fish in the sauce for 4–5 minutes, turning it over once. Add the green part of the spring onions (scallions). Thicken the sauce with the cornflour (cornstarch) paste, sprinkle with the sesame oil and serve.

# STEAMED FISH WITH GINGER AND SPRING ONIONS (SCALLIONS)

*Qing Zheng Yu*

Any firm and delicate fish steaks, such as salmon or turbot, can be cooked by this same method.

SERVES 4–6

**Ingredients**
1 sea bass, trout or grey mullet, weighing about 675g/1½lb, gutted
½ tsp salt
1 tbsp sesame oil
2–3 spring onions (scallions), cut in half lengthways
2 tbsp light soy sauce
2 tbsp Chinese rice wine or dry sherry
1 tbsp finely-shredded fresh ginger
2 tbsp vegetable oil
finely-shredded spring onions (scallions), to garnish

1 Using a sharp knife, score both sides of the fish as far down as the bone with diagonal cuts about 2.5cm/1in apart. Rub the fish all over, inside and out, with salt and sesame oil.

2 Sprinkle the spring onions (scallions) on a heatproof platter and place the fish on top. Blend together the soy sauce and wine or sherry with the ginger shreds and pour evenly all over the fish.

3 Place the platter in a very hot steamer (or inside a wok on a rack), and steam vigorously, under cover, for 12–15 minutes.

4 Heat the oil until hot; remove the platter from the steamer, place the shredded spring onions (scallions) on top of the fish, then pour the hot oil along the whole length of the fish. Serve immediately.

# RED AND WHITE PRAWNS (SHRIMP) WITH GREEN VEGETABLES

## *Yuan Yang Xia*

The Chinese name for this dish is Yuan Yang Prawns (Shrimp). Pairs of mandarin ducks are also known as *yuan yang*, or love birds, because they are always seen together. They often symbolize affection and happiness.

**SERVES 4–6**

**Ingredients**
450g/1lb uncooked prawns (shrimp)
pinch of salt
½ egg white
1 tbsp cornflour (cornstarch) paste
175g/6oz mange-tout (snow peas)
about 575ml/1 pint/2½ cups vegetable oil
½ tsp salt

1 tsp light brown sugar
1 tbsp finely-chopped spring onions (scallions)
1 tsp finely-chopped fresh ginger
1 tbsp light soy sauce
1 tbsp Chinese rice wine or dry sherry
1 tsp chilli bean sauce
1 tbsp tomato purée (paste)

**1** Peel and de-vein the prawns (shrimp), and mix with the pinch of salt, the egg white and the cornflour (cornstarch) paste. Top and tail the mange-tout (snow peas).

**2** Heat about 2–3 tbsp of the oil in a preheated wok and stir-fry the mange-tout (snow peas) for about 1 minute, then add the salt and sugar and continue stirring for another minute. Remove and place in the centre of a serving platter.

**3** Heat the remaining oil, par-cook the prawns (shrimp) for 1 minute, remove and drain.

**4** Pour off the excess oil, leaving about 1 tbsp in the wok, and add the spring onions (scallions) and ginger to flavour the oil.

**5** Add the prawns (shrimp) and stir-fry for about 1 minute, then add the soy sauce and wine or sherry. Blend well and place about half of the prawns (shrimp) at one end of the platter.

**6** Add the chilli bean sauce and tomato purée (paste) to the remaining prawns (shrimp) in the wok, blend well and place the 'red' prawns (shrimp) at the other end of the platter. Serve.

# BAKED LOBSTER WITH BLACK BEANS

*Jiang Cong Guo Long Xia*

The term 'baked', as described on most Chinese restaurant menus, is not strictly correct – 'pot-roasted' or 'pan-baked' is more accurate. Ideally, buy live lobsters and cook them yourself. Ready-cooked ones have usually been boiled for far too long and have lost much of their delicate flavour and texture.

**SERVES 4–6**

**Ingredients**
1 large or 2 medium lobsters, weighing about 800g/1¾lb in total,
vegetable oil, for deep-frying
1 clove garlic, finely chopped
1 tsp finely-chopped fresh ginger
2–3 spring onions (scallions), cut into short sections
2 tbsp black bean sauce
2 tbsp Chinese rice wine or dry sherry
100ml/4fl oz/½ cup Basic Stock
fresh coriander leaves, to garnish

1 Starting from the head, cut the lobster in half lengthways. Discard the legs, remove the claws and crack them with the back of a cleaver. Discard the feathery lungs and intestine. Cut each half into 4–5 pieces.

2 In a wok, deep-fry the lobster pieces in hot oil for about 2 minutes, or until the shells turn bright orange; remove and drain.

3 Pour off the excess oil leaving about 1 tbsp in the wok. Add the garlic, ginger, spring onions (scallions) and black bean sauce.

4 Add the lobster pieces to the sauce and blend well. Add the wine or sherry and stock, bring to the boil and cook for 2–3 minutes under cover. Serve garnished with coriander leaves.

# BAKED CRAB WITH SPRING ONIONS (SCALLIONS) AND GINGER

*Zha Xie*

This recipe is far less complicated to make than it looks. Again, use live crabs if you can for the best flavour and texture.

**SERVES 4**

**Ingredients**

1 large or 2 medium crabs, weighing about
    675g/1½lb in total
2 tbsp Chinese rice wine or dry sherry
1 egg, lightly beaten
1 tbsp cornflour (cornstarch) paste

3–4 tbsp vegetable oil
1 tbsp finely-chopped fresh ginger
3–4 spring onions (scallions), cut into short
    sections
2 tbsp light soy sauce
1 tsp light brown sugar
about 5 tbsp Basic Stock
few drops sesame oil

**1** Cut the crab in half from the underbelly. Break off the claws and crack them with the back of a cleaver. Discard the legs and crack the shell, breaking it into several pieces. Discard the feathery gills and the sac.

**2** Marinate with the wine or sherry, egg and cornflour (cornstarch) for 10–15 minutes.

**3** Heat the oil in a preheated wok and stir-fry the crab pieces with the ginger and spring onions (scallions) for about 2–3 minutes.

**4** Add the soy sauce, sugar and stock, blend well and bring to the boil; braise under cover for 3–4 minutes. Sprinkle with sesame oil and serve.

# CRISPY AND AROMATIC DUCK

*Xiang Cui Ya*

Because this dish is often served with pancakes, spring onions (scallions), cucumber and duck sauce (a sweet bean paste), many people mistakenly think this is the Peking Duck. This recipe however, uses quite a different cooking method. The result is just as crispy but the delightful aroma makes this dish particularly distinctive. Plum sauce may be substituted for the duck sauce.

SERVES 6–8

**Ingredients**
1 oven-ready duckling, weighing about 2–2.3kg/
    4½–5lb
2 tsp salt
5–6 whole star anise
1 tbsp Sichuan peppercorns

1 tsp cloves
2–3 cinnamon sticks
3–4 spring onions (scallions)
3–4 slices fresh ginger, unpeeled
5–6 tbsp Chinese rice wine or dry sherry
vegetable oil, for deep-frying
lettuce leaves, to garnish

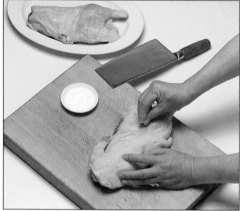

1 Remove the wings from the duck. Split the body in half down the backbone.

2 Rub salt all over the two duck halves taking care to rub it well in.

3 Marinate in a dish with the spices, spring onions (scallions), ginger and wine or sherry for at least 4–6 hours.

4 Vigorously steam the duck with the marinade for 3–4 hours (longer if possible), then remove from the cooking liquid and leave to cool for at least 5–6 hours. The duck must be completely cold and dry or the skin will not be crispy.

5 Heat the oil in a wok until smoking, place the duck pieces in the oil, skin-side down, and deep-fry for 5–6 minutes or until crisp and brown, turning just once at the very last moment.

6 Remove, drain and place on a bed of lettuce leaves. To serve, scrape the meat off the bone and wrap a portion in each pancake with a little sauce, shredded spring onion (scallion) and cucumber. Eat with your fingers.

# FU-YUNG CHICKEN

*Fu Ron Ji*

Because the egg whites (*Fu-yung* in Chinese) mixed with milk are deep-fried, they have prompted some imaginative cooks to refer to this dish as 'Deep-fried Milk'!

**SERVES 4**

**Ingredients**
175g/6oz chicken breast fillet
1 tsp salt
4 egg whites, lightly beaten
1 tbsp cornflour (cornstarch) paste
2 tbsp milk

vegetable oil, for deep-frying
1 lettuce heart, separated into leaves
about 100ml/4fl oz/½ cup Basic Stock
1 tbsp Chinese rice wine or dry sherry
1 tbsp green peas
few drops sesame oil
1 tsp minced (ground) ham, to garnish

1 Finely mince (grind) the chicken meat, then mix with a pinch of the salt, the egg whites, cornflour (cornstarch) paste and milk. Blend well until smooth.

2 Heat the oil in a very hot wok, but before the oil gets too hot, gently spoon the chicken and egg-white mixture into the oil in batches. Do not stir, otherwise it will scatter. Stir the oil from the bottom of the wok so that the *Fu-yung* will rise to the surface. Remove as soon as the colour turns bright white. Drain.

3 Pour off the excess oil, leaving about 1 tbsp in the wok. Stir-fry the lettuce leaves with the remaining salt for 1 minute, add the stock and bring to the boil.

4 Add the chicken to the wok with the wine and peas, and blend well. Sprinkle with the sesame oil and garnish with the ham.

# 'KUNG PO' CHICKEN – SICHUAN STYLE

## *Kung Po Ji Ding*

Kung Po was the name of a court official in Sichuan; his cook created this dish.

**SERVES 4**

**Ingredients**

350g/12oz chicken thigh, boned and skinned
¼ tsp salt
½ egg white, lightly beaten
2 tsp cornflour (cornstarch) paste
1 medium green (bell) pepper, cored and seeded
4 tbsp vegetable oil

3–4 whole dried red chillies, soaked in water for
   10 minutes
1 spring onion (scallion), cut into short sections
few small pieces of fresh ginger, peeled
1 tbsp sweet bean paste or Hoi Sin sauce
1 tsp chilli bean paste
1 tbsp Chinese rice wine or dry sherry
115g/4oz/1 cup roasted cashew nuts
few drops sesame oil

1 Cut the chicken meat into small cubes each about the size of a sugar lump. In a bowl mix together with the salt, egg white and the cornflour (cornstarch) paste.

2 Cut the green (bell) pepper into cubes about the same size as the chicken.

3 Heat the oil in a preheated wok. Stir-fry the chicken cubes for about 1 minute, or until the colour changes, remove with a perforated spoon and keep warm.

4 Add the green (bell) pepper, dried red chillies, spring onion (scallion) and ginger and stir-fry for about 1 minute; then add the chicken with the bean pastes or sauce and wine or sherry. Blend well and cook for another minute. Finally add the cashew nuts and sesame oil. Serve hot.

# PEKING DUCK

*Bei Jing Ya*

This has to be the *pièce de résistance* of any Chinese banquet. It is not too difficult to prepare and cook at home – the secret is to use duckling with a low fat content. Also, make sure that the skin of the duck is absolutely dry before cooking – the drier the skin, the crispier the duck.

SERVES 6–8

**Ingredients**
1 oven-ready duckling, weighing about 2.3–2.5kg/ 5–5½lb
2 tbsp maltose or honey, dissolved in 150ml/ ¼ pint/⅔ cup warm water

**For serving**
20–24 Thin Pancakes
100ml/4fl oz/½ cup Duck Sauce (see below) or plum sauce
6–8 spring onions (scallions), thinly shredded
½ cucumber, thinly shredded

### Duck Sauce

To make Duck Sauce, heat 2 tbsp sesame oil in a small saucepan. Add 6–8 tbsp crushed yellow bean sauce and 2–3 tbsp light brown sugar. Stir until smooth and allow to cool. Serve cold.

1 Remove any feather studs and any lumps of fat from inside the vent of the duck. Plunge the duck into a pot of boiling water for 2–3 minutes to seal the pores. This will make the skin air-tight, thus preventing the fat from escaping during cooking. Remove and drain well, then dry thoroughly.

2 Brush the duck all over with the dissolved maltose or honey, then hang the duck up in a cool place for at least 4–5 hours.

3 Place the duck, breast side up, on a rack in a roasting pan, and cook in a preheated oven (200°C/400°F/Gas Mark 6) for 1½–1¾ hours without basting or turning.

4 To serve, peel off the crispy duck skin in small slices using a sharp carving knife or cleaver, then carve the juicy meat in thin strips. Arrange the skin and meat on separate serving plates.

5 Open a pancake on each plate, spread about 1 tsp of sauce in the middle, with a few strips of shredded spring onions (scallions) and cucumber. Top with 2–3 slices each of duck skin and meat.

# SHREDDED CHICKEN WITH CELERY

*Qing Cai Chao Ji Si*

The tender chicken breast contrasts with the crunchy texture of the celery, and the red chillies add colour and flavour.

| SERVES 4 | ½ egg white, lightly beaten | I spring onion (scallion), thinly shredded |
|---|---|---|
| | 2 tsp cornflour (cornstarch) paste | few strips fresh ginger, thinly shredded |
| **Ingredients** | about 500ml/16 fl oz/2 cups vegetable oil | I tsp light brown sugar |
| 285g/10oz chicken breast fillet | I celery heart, thinly shredded | I tbsp Chinese rice wine or dry sherry |
| I tsp salt | I–2 fresh red chillies, seeded and thinly shredded | few drops sesame oil |

1 Using a sharp knife, thinly shred the chicken. In a bowl, mix together with a pinch of the salt, the egg white, and the cornflour (cornstarch) paste.

2 Heat the oil in a wok until warm, add the chicken and stir to separate the shreds. When the chicken turns white, remove with a strainer and drain. Keep warm.

3 In 2 tbsp of oil, stir-fry the celery, chillies, spring onion (scallion) and ginger for 1 minute. Add the chicken, salt, sugar and wine. Cook for 1 minute and add the sesame oil. Serve hot.

# CHICKEN WITH CHINESE VEGETABLES

*Ji Pian Chao Shi Cai*

The chicken can be replaced by almost any other meat, such as pork, beef, liver or prawns (shrimp).

| SERVES 4 | 2 tsp cornflour (cornstarch) paste | I spring onion (scallion), cut into short sections |
|---|---|---|
| | 4 tbsp vegetable oil | few small pieces fresh ginger, peeled |
| **Ingredients** | 6–8 small dried Chinese mushrooms (shiitake), soaked | I tsp light brown sugar |
| 225–285g/8–10oz chicken, boned and skinned | 115g/4oz sliced bamboo shoots, drained | I tbsp light soy sauce |
| I tsp salt | 115g/4oz mange-tout (snow peas), trimmed | I tbsp Chinese rice wine or dry sherry |
| ½ egg white, lightly beaten | | few drops sesame oil |

1 Cut the chicken into thin slices each about the size of an oblong postage stamp. In a bowl, mix with a pinch of the salt, the egg white and the cornflour (cornstarch) paste.

2 Heat the oil in a preheated wok, stir-fry the chicken over medium heat for about 30 seconds, then remove with a perforated spoon and keep warm.

3 Stir-fry the vegetables over high heat for about 1 minute. Add the salt, sugar and chicken. Blend, then add the soy sauce and wine or sherry. Stir a few more times. Sprinkle with the sesame oil and serve.

# SOY-BRAISED CHICKEN

*Jiang You Ji*

This dish can be served hot or cold as part of a buffet-style meal.

**SERVES 6–8**

**Ingredients**
1 whole chicken, weighing about 1.35–1.5kg/
  3–3½lb
1 tbsp ground Sichuan peppercorns
2 tbsp minced (ground) fresh ginger
3 tbsp light soy sauce

2 tbsp dark soy sauce
3 tbsp Chinese rice wine or dry sherry
1 tbsp light brown sugar
vegetable oil, for deep-frying
about 575ml/1 pint/2½ cups Basic Stock or water
2 tsp salt
25g/1oz rock (crystal) sugar
lettuce leaves, to garnish

1 Rub the chicken both inside and out with the ground pepper and fresh ginger. Marinate the bird with the soy sauces, wine or sherry and sugar for at least 3 hours, turning it several times.

2 Heat the oil in a preheated wok, remove the chicken from the marinade and deep-fry for 5–6 minutes, or until brown all over. Remove and drain.

3 Pour off the excess oil, add the marinade with the stock or water, salt and rock (crystal) sugar and bring to the boil. Braise the chicken in the sauce for 35–40 minutes under cover, turning once or twice.

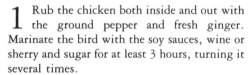

4 Remove the chicken from the wok and let it cool down a little before chopping it into approximately 30 bite-sized pieces. Arrange the pieces on a bed of lettuce leaves, then pour some of the sauce over the chicken and serve. The remains of the sauce can be stored in the refrigerator to be re-used again and again.

# CHICKEN AND HAM WITH GREEN VEGETABLES

*Jin Hua Yi Shu Ji*

The Chinese name for this colourful dish means 'Golden Flower and Jade Tree Chicken'. It makes a marvellous buffet-style dish for all occasions.

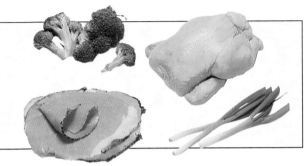

**SERVES 6–8**

**Ingredients**
1 whole chicken weighing about 1–1.35kg/
 2¼–3lb
2 spring onions (scallions)
2–3 pieces fresh ginger

1 tbsp salt
225g/8oz honey-roast ham
285g/10oz broccoli
3 tbsp vegetable oil
1 tsp light brown sugar
2 tsp cornflour (cornstarch)

1 Place the chicken in a large pan and cover it with cold water. Add the spring onions (scallions), ginger and about 2 tsp of the salt. Bring to the boil, then reduce the heat and simmer for 10–15 minutes under a tightly-fitting cover. Turn off the heat and let the chicken cook itself in the hot water for at least 4–5 hours – you must not lift up the cover, as this will let out the residual heat.

2 Remove the chicken from the pan, reserving the liquid, and carefully cut the meat away from the bones, keeping the skin on. Slice both the chicken and ham into pieces, each the size of a matchbox, and arrange the meats in alternating layers on a plate.

3 Cut the broccoli into small florets and stir-fry in the hot oil with the remaining salt and the sugar for about 2–3 minutes. Arrange the vegetables between the rows of chicken and ham and around the edge of the plate, making a border for the meat.

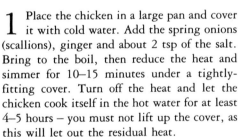

4 Heat a small amount of the chicken stock and thicken with the cornflour (cornstarch). Stir until smooth, then pour it evenly all over the chicken and ham so that it forms a thin coat of transparent jelly resembling 'jade'. Allow to cool before serving.

# MU SHU PORK WITH EGGS AND WOOD-EARS

*Mu Shu Rou*

Mu Shu is the Chinese name for a bright yellow flower. Traditionally, this dish is served as a filling wrapped in thin pancakes, but it can also be served on its own with plain rice.

**SERVES 4**

**Ingredients**
15g/½oz dried black fungus (wood-ears)
175–225g/6–8oz pork fillet
225g/8oz Chinese leaves
115g/4oz bamboo shoots, drained
2 spring onions (scallions)
3 eggs
1 tsp salt
4 tbsp vegetable oil
1 tbsp light soy sauce
1 tbsp Chinese rice wine or dry sherry
few drops sesame oil

1 Soak the fungus in cold water for 25–30 minutes, rinse and discard the hard stalks, if any. Drain, then thinly shred.

2 Cut the pork into matchstick-size shreds. Thinly shred the Chinese leaves, bamboo shoots and spring onions (scallions).

3 Beat the eggs with a pinch of the salt and lightly scramble in a little of the warm oil until set, but not too dry. Remove.

4 Heat the remaining oil in the wok and stir-fry the pork for about 1 minute, or until the colour changes.

5 Add the vegetables to the wok, stir-fry for another minute, then add the remaining salt, the soy sauce and wine or sherry.

6 Stir for 1 more minute before adding the scrambled eggs. Break up the scrambled eggs and blend well. Sprinkle with sesame oil and serve.

# STUFFED GREEN (BELL) PEPPERS

*Niang Qing Chaio*

Ideally, use small, thin-skinned green (bell) peppers for this recipe.

**SERVES 4**

**Ingredients**
225–285g/8–10oz minced (ground) pork
4–6 water chestnuts, finely chopped
2 spring onions (scallions), finely chopped
½ tsp finely-chopped fresh ginger
1 tbsp light soy sauce
1 tbsp Chinese rice wine or dry sherry
3–4 green (bell) peppers, cored and seeded

1 tbsp cornflour (cornstarch)
vegetable oil, for deep-frying

**Sauce**
2 tsp light soy sauce
1 tsp light brown sugar
1–2 fresh hot chillies, finely chopped (optional)
about 5 tbsp Basic Stock or water

1 In a bowl, mix the minced (ground) pork with the water chestnuts, spring onions (scallions), ginger, soy sauce and wine or sherry.

2 Halve or quarter the green (bell) peppers. Stuff the sections with the pork mixture and sprinkle with a little cornflour (cornstarch).

3 Heat the oil in a preheated wok and deep-fry the stuffed (bell) peppers, with the meat-side down, for 2–3 minutes, then remove and drain.

4 Pour off the excess oil, then return the stuffed green (bell) peppers to the wok with the meat-side up. Add the sauce ingredients, shaking the wok gently to make sure they do not stick to the bottom, and braise for 2–3 minutes. Carefully lift the stuffed peppers onto a serving dish, meat-side up, and pour the sauce over them. Serve.

# TWICE-COOKED PORK – SICHUAN STYLE

*Hui Guo Rou*

Any left-overs from a roast joint of pork can be used for this dish.

**SERVES 4**

**Ingredients**
225g/8oz shoulder or knuckle of pork
1 small green (bell) pepper, cored and seeded
115g/4oz sliced bamboo shoots, rinsed and
   drained
1 spring onion (scallion)
3 tbsp vegetable oil
1 tsp salt
½ tsp light brown sugar
1 tbsp yellow bean sauce
1 tsp chilli bean sauce
1 tbsp Chinese rice wine or dry sherry

1 Immerse the whole piece of pork into a pot of boiling water, return to the boil and skim the surface. Reduce the heat and simmer, covered, for 25–30 minutes. Turn off the heat and leave the pork in the water, covered, to cool, for at least 3–4 hours before removing.

2 Trim off and remove any excess fat from the pork and cut the meat into thin slices, each about the size of a large postage stamp. Cut the green (bell) peppers into pieces the size of the bamboo shoots and cut the spring onion (scallion) into short sections.

3 Heat the oil in a preheated wok, add the green (bell) pepper, the spring onion (scallion) and bamboo shoots, and stir-fry for about 1 minute.

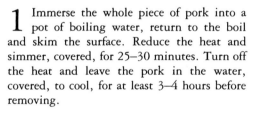

4 Add the pork followed by the salt, sugar, yellow bean sauce, chilli bean sauce and wine or sherry. Continue stirring for a further 1–2 minutes. Serve.

# SWEET AND SOUR PORK

*Tang Cu Gu Luo Rou*

Sweet and Sour Pork must be one of the most popular dishes served in Chinese restaurants and take-aways in the Western world. Unfortunately, it is too often spoiled by cooks who use too much tomato ketchup in the sauce. Here is a classic recipe from Canton, the city of its origin.

| | | |
|---|---|---|
| **SERVES 4** | 2 tbsp plain (all-purpose) flour | 1 small green (bell) pepper, cut into small cubes |
| | 1 egg, lightly beaten | 1 fresh red chilli, seeded and thinly shredded |
| **Ingredients** | vegetable oil, for deep-frying | 1 tbsp light soy sauce |
| 350g/12oz lean pork | | 2 tbsp light brown sugar |
| ¼ tsp salt | **Sauce** | 2–3 tbsp rice vinegar |
| ½ tsp ground Sichuan peppercorns | 1 tbsp vegetable oil | 1 tbsp tomato purée (paste) |
| 1 tbsp Chinese rice wine or dry sherry | 1 clove garlic, finely chopped | about 100ml/4fl oz/½ cup Basic Stock or water |
| 115g/4oz bamboo shoots | 1 spring onion (scallion), cut into short sections | |

1 Cut the pork into small bite-sized cubes. Marinate with the salt, pepper and wine or sherry for 15–20 minutes.

2 Cut the bamboo shoots into small cubes the same size as the pork.

3 Dust the pork with flour, dip in the beaten egg, and coat with more flour. Deep-fry in moderately hot oil for 3–4 minutes, stirring to separate the pieces. Remove.

4 Reheat the oil to hot, add the pork and bamboo shoots and fry for about 1 minute or until golden. Remove and drain.

5 Heat the oil and add the garlic, spring onion (scallion), green (bell) pepper and red chilli. Stir-fry for 30–40 seconds, then add the seasoning with the stock. Bring to the boil, then add the pork and bamboo shoots.

# STIR-FRIED PORK WITH VEGETABLES I

*Rou Pian Chao Shucai*

This is a basic recipe for cooking any meat with any vegetables, according to seasonal availability.

---

**SERVES 4**

**Ingredients**
225g/8oz pork fillet
I tbsp light soy sauce
I tsp light brown sugar

I tsp Chinese rice wine or dry sherry
2 tsp cornflour (cornstarch) paste
115g/4oz mange-tout (snow peas)
115g/4oz white mushrooms
I medium or 2 small carrots
I spring onion (scallion)

4 tbsp vegetable oil
I tsp salt
Basic Stock or water, if necessary
few drops sesame oil

---

1 Cut the pork into thin slices each about the size of an oblong postage stamp. Marinate with about 1 tsp of the soy sauce, sugar, wine or sherry and cornflour (cornstarch) paste.

2 Top and tail the mange-tout (snow peas); thinly slice the mushrooms; cut the carrots into pieces roughly the same size as the pork, and cut the spring onion (scallion) into short sections.

3 Heat the oil in a preheated wok and stir-fry the pork for about 1 minute or until its colour changes. Remove with a perforated spoon and keep warm.

4 Stir-fry the vegetables for about 2 minutes, add the salt and the partly-cooked pork, and a little stock or water only if necessary. Continue stirring for another minute or so, then add the remaining soy sauce and blend well. Sprinkle with the sesame oil and serve.

# LION'S HEAD CASSEROLE

*Shi Zi Tou*

The meatballs are supposed to resemble a lion's head, and the Chinese leaves its mane, hence the dish's name.

---

SERVES 4–6

**Ingredients**
450g/1lb minced (ground) pork
2 tsp finely-chopped spring onions (scallions)
1 tsp finely-chopped fresh ginger
50g/2oz white mushrooms, finely chopped
50g/2oz peeled prawns (shrimp) or crabmeat, finely chopped
1 tbsp light soy sauce
1 tsp light brown sugar
1 tbsp Chinese rice wine or dry sherry
1 tbsp cornflour (cornstarch)
675g/1½lb Chinese leaves
3–4 tbsp vegetable oil
1 tsp salt
about 300ml/½ pint/1¼ cups Basic Stock or water

---

1 Mix the pork with the spring onions (scallions), ginger, mushrooms, prawns (shrimp), soy sauce, sugar, wine and cornflour (cornstarch). Shape into 4–6 meatballs.

2 Cut the Chinese leaves into large pieces, all roughly the same size.

3 Heat the oil and stir-fry the Chinese leaves with the salt for 2–3 minutes. Add the meatballs and the stock, bring to the boil, cover and simmer gently for 30–45 minutes.

---

# STIR-FRIED PORK WITH VEGETABLES II

*Rou Pian Chao Shucai*

In this simple, colourful dish, the courgettes (zucchini) can be replaced by cucumber or green (bell) peppers.

---

SERVES 4

**Ingredients**
225g/8oz pork fillet, thinly sliced
1 tbsp light soy sauce
1 tsp light brown sugar
1 tsp Chinese rice wine or dry sherry
2 tsp cornflour (cornstarch) paste
115g/4oz firm tomatoes, peeled
175g/6oz courgettes (zucchini)
1 spring onion (scallion)
4 tbsp vegetable oil
1 tsp salt (optional)
Basic Stock or water, if necessary

---

1 In a bowl, marinate the pork with about 1 tsp of the soy sauce, the sugar, wine and cornflour (cornstarch) paste. Cut the tomatoes and courgettes (zucchini) into wedges and the spring onion (scallion) into sections.

2 Heat the oil in a preheated wok and stir-fry the pork for about 1 minute or until the colour changes. Remove with a perforated spoon and keep warm.

3 Stir-fry the vegetables for about 2 minutes, add the salt if using, the pork and a little stock or water. Stir for another minute or so, then add the remaining soy sauce and blend well. Serve.

# BEEF AND LAMB DISHES

# SWEET AND SOUR LAMB

*Tang Cu Yang Rou*

This recipe from the Imperial kitchens of the Manchu Dynasty is perhaps a forerunner of Sweet and Sour Pork.

| SERVES 4 | vegetable oil, for deep-frying | 2 tbsp light brown sugar |
|---|---|---|
| | ½ tsp finely-chopped fresh ginger | 3–4 tbsp Basic Stock or water |
| **Ingredients** | 1 tbsp light soy sauce | 1 tbsp cornflour (cornstarch) paste |
| 350–400g/12–14oz leg of lamb fillet | 1 tbsp Chinese rice wine or dry sherry | ½ tsp sesame oil |
| 1 tbsp yellow bean sauce | 2 tbsp rice vinegar | |

1 Cut the lamb into thin slices each about the size of an oblong postage stamp. In a bowl, marinate the lamb with the yellow bean sauce for 35–40 minutes.

2 In a wok, deep-fry the lamb in the hot oil for about 30–40 seconds or until the colour changes. Remove with a perforated spoon and drain.

3 Pour off the excess oil, leaving about ½ tbsp in the wok. Add the ginger and the remaining ingredients and stir until smooth. Add the lamb, blend well and serve.

# STIR-FRIED LAMB WITH SPRING ONIONS (SCALLIONS)

*Cong Bao Yang Rou*

This is a classic Beijing 'meat and veg' recipe, in which the lamb can be replaced with either beef or pork, and the spring onions (scallions) by other strongly-flavoured vegetables, such as leeks or onions.

| SERVES 4 | 1 tbsp light soy sauce | about 300ml/½ pint/1¼ cups vegetable oil |
|---|---|---|
| | 1 tbsp Chinese rice wine or dry sherry | few small pieces fresh ginger |
| **Ingredients** | 2 tsp cornflour (cornstarch) paste | 2 tbsp yellow bean sauce |
| 350–400g/12–14 oz leg of lamb fillet | 15g/½oz dried black fungus (wood-ears) | few drops sesame oil |
| 1 tsp light brown sugar | 6–8 spring onions (scallions) | |

1 Slice the lamb thinly. Marinate with the sugar, soy sauce, wine and cornflour (cornstarch) paste for 30–45 minutes. Soak the fungus for 25–30 minutes, then cut into small pieces with the spring onions (scallions).

2 Heat the oil in a preheated wok until hot and stir-fry the meat for about 1 minute, or until the colour changes. Remove with a perforated spoon and drain.

3 Keep about 1 tbsp of oil in the wok, then add the spring onions (scallions), ginger, fungus and yellow bean sauce. Blend well, then add the meat and stir for about 1 minute. Sprinkle with the sesame oil.

# DRY-FRIED SHREDDED BEEF

*Gan Shao Niu Rou*

Dry-frying is a unique Sichuan cooking method, in which the main ingredient is firstly stir-fried slowly over a low heat until dry, then finished off quickly with other ingredients over a high heat.

**SERVES 4**

**Ingredients**
350–400g/12–14oz beef steak
1 large or 2 small carrots
2–3 stalks celery
2 tbsp sesame oil
1 tbsp Chinese rice wine or dry sherry

1 tbsp chilli bean sauce
1 tbsp light soy sauce
1 clove garlic, finely chopped
1 tsp light brown sugar
2–3 spring onions (scallions), finely chopped
½ tsp finely-chopped fresh ginger
ground Sichuan peppercorns, to taste

1 Cut the beef into matchstick-size strips. Thinly shred the carrots and celery.

2 Heat the sesame oil in a preheated wok (it will smoke very quickly). Reduce the heat and stir-fry the beef shreds with the wine or sherry until the colour changes.

3 Pour off the excess liquid and reserve. Continue stirring until the meat is absolutely dry.

4 Add the chilli bean sauce, soy sauce, garlic and sugar; blend well, then add the carrot and celery shreds. Increase the heat to high and add the spring onions (scallions), ginger and the reserved liquid. Continue stirring, and when all the juice has evaporated, season with Sichuan pepper and serve.

# BEEF WITH CANTONESE OYSTER SAUCE

*Hao You Niu Rou*

This is a classic Cantonese recipe in which any combination of vegetables can be used. Broccoli may be used instead of mange-tout (snow peas), bamboo shoots instead of baby corn cobs, and white or black mushrooms instead of straw mushrooms, for example.

SERVES 4

**Ingredients**
285–350g/10–12oz beef steak
1 tsp light brown sugar
1 tbsp light soy sauce
2 tsp Chinese rice wine or dry sherry
2 tsp cornflour (cornstarch) paste

115g/4oz mange-tout (snow peas)
115g/4oz baby corn cobs
115g/4oz canned straw mushrooms, drained
1 spring onion (scallion)
300ml/½ pint/1¼ cups vegetable oil
few small pieces fresh ginger
½ tsp salt
2 tbsp oyster sauce

1 Cut the beef into thin slices each about the size of an oblong postage stamp. In a bowl, marinate the beef with the sugar, soy sauce, wine or sherry and cornflour (cornstarch) paste for 25–30 minutes.

2 Top and tail the mange-tout (snow peas); cut the baby corn cobs in half and also the straw mushrooms if large, but leave whole if small. Cut the spring onion (scallion) into short sections.

3 Heat the oil in a preheated wok and stir-fry the beef until the colour changes. Remove with a perforated spoon and drain.

4 Pour off the excess oil, leaving about 2 tbsp in the wok, then add the spring onion (scallion), ginger and the vegetables. Stir-fry for about 2 minutes with the salt, then add the beef and the oyster sauce. Blend well and serve.

# STIR-FRIED MIXED VEGETABLES I

*Su Shi Jin*

Black or oyster mushrooms may be used in place of the white mushrooms in this dish.

| SERVES 4 | 115g/4oz white mushrooms | Basic Stock or water, if necessary |
|---|---|---|
| **Ingredients** | 1 medium red (bell) pepper, cored and seeded | 1 tbsp light soy sauce |
| 115g/4oz mange-tout (snow peas) | 4 tbsp vegetable oil | few drops sesame oil (optional) |
| 115g/4oz courgettes (zucchini) | 1 tsp salt | |
| | 1 tsp light brown sugar | |

1 Cut the vegetables into roughly similar shapes and sizes. Top and tail the mange-tout (snow peas) and leave whole if small, otherwise cut in half.

2 Heat the oil in a wok and stir-fry the vegetables for about 2 minutes.

3 Add the salt and sugar, and a little stock or water *only* if necessary, and stir for 1 minute. Finally add the soy sauce and sesame oil, if using. Blend well and serve.

# STIR-FRIED MIXED VEGETABLES II

*Su Shi Jin*

When selecting different items for a dish, never mix ingredients indiscriminately. The idea is to achieve a harmonious balance of colour and texture.

| SERVES 4 | 115g/4oz broccoli | Basic Stock or water, if necessary |
|---|---|---|
| **Ingredients** | 1 medium or 2 small carrots | 1 tbsp light soy sauce |
| 225g/8oz Chinese leaves | 4 tbsp vegetable oil | few drops sesame oil (optional) |
| 115g/4oz baby corn cobs | 1 tsp salt | |
| | 1 tsp light brown sugar | |

1 Cut the vegetables into roughly similar shapes and sizes.

2 Heat the oil in a wok and stir-fry the vegetables for about 2 minutes.

3 Add the salt and sugar, and a little stock or water *only* if necessary, and continue stirring for another minute. Add the soy sauce and sesame oil, if using. Blend well and serve.

# SICHUAN SPICY BEAN CURD (TOFU)

*Ma Po Dao Fu*

This universally popular dish originated in Sichuan in the nineteenth century. The meat used in the recipe can be omitted to create a purely vegetarian dish.

**SERVES 4**

**Ingredients**
3 cakes bean curd (tofu)
1 leek
115g/4oz minced (ground) beef
3 tbsp vegetable oil
1 tbsp black bean sauce

1 tbsp light soy sauce
1 tsp chilli bean sauce
1 tbsp Chinese rice wine or dry sherry
about 3–4 tbsp Basic Stock or water
2 tsp cornflour (cornstarch) paste
ground Sichuan peppercorns, to taste
few drops sesame oil

1 Cut the bean curd (tofu) into 1cm/½in square cubes; blanch the cubes in a pan of boiling water for 2–3 minutes to harden. Remove and drain. Cut the leek into short sections.

2 Stir-fry the minced (ground) beef in oil until the colour changes, then add the leek and black bean sauce. Add the bean curd (tofu) with the soy sauce, chilli bean sauce and wine or sherry. Stir gently for 1 minute.

3 Add the stock or water, bring to the boil and braise for 2–3 minutes.

4 Thicken the sauce with the cornflour (cornstarch) paste, season with the ground Sichuan pepper and sprinkle with the sesame oil. Serve.

# YU HSIANG AUBERGINE (EGGPLANT) IN SPICY SAUCE

*Yu Hsiang Gai*

*Yu Hsiang*, which literally means 'fish fragrance', is a Sichuan cookery term indicating that the dish is cooked with seasonings originally used in fish dishes.

SERVES 4

**Ingredients**
450g/1lb aubergines (eggplant)
3–4 whole dried red chillies, soaked in water
  for 10 minutes
vegetable oil, for deep-frying
1 clove garlic, finely chopped

1 tsp finely-chopped fresh ginger
1 tsp finely-chopped spring onion (scallion),
  white part only
115g/4oz lean pork, thinly shredded (optional)
1 tbsp light soy sauce
1 tsp light brown sugar
1 tbsp chilli bean sauce
1 tbsp Chinese rice wine or dry sherry

1 tbsp rice vinegar
2 tsp cornflour (cornstarch) paste
1 tsp finely-chopped spring onions (scallions),
  green part only, to garnish
few drops sesame oil

1 Cut the aubergines (eggplant) into short strips the size of chips (French fries) – the skin can either be peeled or left on, whichever you prefer. Cut the soaked red chillies into 2–3 small pieces and discard the seeds.

2 In a wok, heat the oil and deep-fry the aubergine (eggplant) 'chips' for about 3–4 minutes or until limp. Remove and drain.

3 Pour off the excess oil, leaving about 1 tbsp in the wok. Add the garlic, ginger, white spring onions (scallions) and chillies, stir a few times then add the pork, if using. Stir-fry the meat for about 1 minute or until the colour changes to pale white. Add all the seasonings, then bring to the boil.

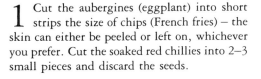

4 Add the aubergines (eggplant) to the wok, blend well and braise for 30–40 seconds, then thicken the sauce with the cornflour (cornstarch) paste, stirring until smooth. Garnish with the green spring onions (scallions) and sprinkle with the sesame oil.

### Cook's tip

Soaking dried chillies in water will reduce their spicy flavour. If you prefer a milder chilli taste, soak for longer than the recommended 10 minutes.

## BROCCOLI IN OYSTER SAUCE

### Hao You Xi Lan

Vegetarians may prefer to replace oyster sauce with soy sauce.

---

**SERVES 4**

**Ingredients**
450g/1lb broccoli
3–4 tbsp vegetable oil
½ tsp salt
½ tsp light brown sugar
2–3 tbsp Basic Stock or water
2 tbsp oyster sauce

---

1 Cut the broccoli heads into florets; remove the rough skin from the stalks, and diagonally slice the florets into diamond-shaped chunks.

2 Heat the oil in a preheated wok and add the salt, then stir-fry the broccoli for about 2 minutes. Add the sugar and stock or water, and continue stirring for another minute. Finally add the oyster sauce, blend well and serve.

## STIR-FRIED CHINESE LEAVES WITH MUSHROOMS

### Pia Cai Cao Gu

You can also use fresh button mushrooms for this recipe.

---

**SERVES 4**

**Ingredients**
225g/8oz fresh straw mushrooms or 1 350g/12oz can straw mushrooms, drained
4 tbsp vegetable oil
400g/14oz Chinese leaves, cut in strips
1 tsp salt
1 tsp light brown sugar
1 tbsp cornflour (cornstarch) paste
100ml/4fl oz/½ cup milk

---

1 Cut the mushrooms in half lengthways. Heat half the oil, stir-fry the Chinese leaves for 2 minutes, then add half the salt and half the sugar. Stir for 1 minute, then place on a dish.

2 Stir-fry the mushrooms for 1 minute. Add salt and sugar, cook for 1 minute, then thicken with the cornflour (cornstarch) paste and milk. Serve with the greens.

## STIR-FRIED BEAN SPROUTS

### Chao Dao Ya

It is not necessary to top and tail the bean sprouts for this quick and simple recipe. Simply rinse in a bowl of cold water, and discard any husks that float to the surface.

---

**SERVES 4**

**Ingredients**
2–3 spring onions (scallions)
225g/8oz fresh bean sprouts
3 tbsp vegetable oil
1 tsp salt
½ tsp light brown sugar
few drops sesame oil (optional)

---

1 Cut the spring onions (scallions) into short sections about the same length as the bean sprouts.

2 Heat the oil in a wok and stir-fry the bean sprouts and spring onions (scallions) for about 1 minute. Add the salt and sugar and continue stirring for another minute. Sprinkle with the sesame oil, if using, and serve. Do not over-cook, or the sprouts will go soggy.

# BRAISED CHINESE VEGETABLES

*Lo Han Zhai*

The original recipe calls for no less than 18 different ingredients to represent the 18 Buddhas (*Lo Han*). Later, this was reduced to eight, but nowadays anything between four and six items is regarded as quite sufficient.

**SERVES 4**

**Ingredients**
7g/¼oz dried black fungus (wood-ears)
85g/3oz straw mushrooms, drained
85g/3oz sliced bamboo shoots, drained
50g/2oz mange-tout (snow peas)
1 cake bean curd (tofu)
175g/6oz Chinese leaves

3–4 tbsp vegetable oil
1 tsp salt
½ tsp light brown sugar
1 tbsp light soy sauce
few drops sesame oil (optional)

1 Soak the black fungus in cold water for 20–25 minutes, then rinse and discard the hard stalks, if any. Cut the straw mushrooms in half lengthways, if large – keep them whole, if small. Rinse and drain the bamboo shoot slices. Top and tail the mange-tout (snow peas). Cut the bean curd (tofu) into about 12 small pieces. Cut the Chinese leaves into small pieces about the same size as the mange-tout (snow peas).

2 Harden the bean curd (tofu) pieces by placing them in a pan of boiling water for about 2 minutes. Remove and drain.

3 Heat the oil in a flameproof casserole or saucepan and lightly brown the bean curd (tofu) pieces on both sides. Remove with a slotted spoon and keep warm.

4 Stir-fry all the vegetables in the casserole or saucepan for about 1½ minutes, then add the bean curd (tofu) pieces, salt, sugar and soy sauce. Continue stirring for another minute, then cover and braise for 2–3 minutes. Sprinkle with sesame oil (if using) and serve.

# BAMBOO SHOOTS AND CHINESE MUSHROOMS

## *Chao Shang Dong*

Another name for this dish is 'Twin Winter Vegetables', because both bamboo shoots and mushrooms are at their best during the winter season. For that reason, try using canned winter bamboo shoots and extra 'fat' mushrooms.

| SERVES 4 | 285g/10oz winter bamboo shoots | 1 tbsp Chinese rice wine or dry sherry |
| --- | --- | --- |
| | 3 tbsp vegetable oil | ½ tsp light brown sugar |
| **Ingredients** | 1 spring onion (scallion), cut into short sections | 2 tsp cornflour (cornstarch) paste |
| 50g/2oz dried Chinese mushrooms (shiitake) | 2 tbsp light soy sauce or oyster sauce | few drops sesame oil |

1 Soak the mushrooms in cold water for at least 3 hours, then squeeze dry and discard any hard stalks, reserving the water. Cut the mushrooms in half, or quarters if they are large – keep them whole if small.

2 Rinse and drain the bamboo shoots, then cut them into small, wedge-shaped pieces.

3 Heat the oil in a preheated wok and stir-fry the mushrooms and bamboo shoots for about 1 minute. Add the spring onion (scallion) and seasonings with about 2–3 tbsp of the mushroom water. Bring to the boil and braise for another minute or so, then thicken the gravy with the cornflour (cornstarch) paste and sprinkle with the sesame oil.

# STIR-FRIED TOMATOES, CUCUMBER AND EGGS

## *Chao San Wei*

The cucumber can be replaced by a green (bell) pepper or courgette (zucchini) if preferred.

| SERVES 4 | ⅓ cucumber, unpeeled | 4 tbsp vegetable oil |
| --- | --- | --- |
| | 4 eggs | 2 tsp Chinese rice wine or dry sherry (optional) |
| **Ingredients** | 1 tsp salt | |
| 175g/6oz firm tomatoes, peeled | 1 spring onion (scallion), finely chopped | |

1 Halve the tomatoes and cucumber, then cut across into small wedges. In a bowl, beat the eggs with a pinch of the salt and a few pieces of the spring onion (scallion).

2 Heat about half of the oil in a preheated wok, then lightly scramble the eggs over a moderate heat until set, but not too dry. Remove and keep warm.

3 Heat the remaining oil over a high heat, add the vegetables and stir-fry for 1 minute. Add the remaining salt, then the scrambled eggs and wine or sherry, if using.

# RICE, NOODLES AND DIM SUM

# NOODLES IN SOUP

## *Tang Mein*

In China, noodles in soup (*Tang Mein*) are far more popular than Fried Noodles (*Chow Mein*). This is a basic recipe which you can adapt by using different ingredients for the 'dressing'.

**SERVES 4**

**Ingredients**
225g/8oz chicken breast fillet, pork fillet, or
    ready-cooked meat
3–4 Chinese dried mushrooms (shiitake), soaked
115g/4oz sliced bamboo shoots, drained
115g/4oz spinach leaves, lettuce hearts, or
    Chinese leaves
2 spring onions (scallions)
350g/12oz dried egg noodles
575ml/1 pint/2½ cups Basic Stock
2 tbsp vegetable oil
1 tsp salt
½ tsp light brown sugar
1 tbsp light soy sauce

2 tsp Chinese rice wine or dry sherry
few drops sesame oil

1 Thinly shred the meat. Squeeze dry the mushrooms and discard any hard stalks. Thinly shred the mushrooms, bamboo shoots, greens and spring onions (scallions).

2 Cook the noodles in boiling water according to the instructions on the packet, then drain and rinse under cold water. Place in a serving bowl.

3 Bring the stock to the boil and pour over the noodles; keep warm.

4 Heat the oil in a preheated wok, add about half of the spring onions (scallions) and the meat, and stir-fry for about 1 minute.

5 Add the mushrooms, bamboo shoots and greens and stir-fry for 1 minute. Add all the seasonings and blend well.

6 Pour the 'dressing' over the noodles, garnish with the remaining spring onions (scallions) and serve.

# PLAIN RICE

*Pai Fan*

Use long grain or patna rice, or fragrant rice from Thailand. Allow 50–55g/2oz/⅓ cup raw rice per person.

| SERVES 4 | about 250ml/8fl oz/1 cup cold water |
| --- | --- |
| | pinch of salt |
| **Ingredients** | ½ tsp vegetable oil |
| 225g/8oz/1⅓ cups rice | |

1 Wash and rinse the rice. Place the rice in a saucepan and add the water. There should be no more than 2cm/⅔in of water above the surface of the rice.

2 Bring to the boil, add the salt and oil, then stir to prevent the rice sticking to the bottom of the pan. Reduce the heat to very, very low and cook for 15–20 minutes, covered.

3 Remove from the heat and leave to stand for 10 minutes. Fluff up the rice with a fork or spoon just before serving.

# EGG FRIED RICE

*Dan Chao Fan*

Use rice with a fairly firm texture. Ideally, the raw rice should be soaked in water for a short time before cooking.

| SERVES 4 | 2–3 tbsp vegetable oil |
| --- | --- |
| | 450g/1lb cooked rice |
| **Ingredients** | 115g/4oz green peas |
| 3 eggs | |
| 1 tsp salt | |
| 2 spring onions (scallions), finely chopped | |

1 In a bowl, lightly beat the eggs with a pinch of the salt and a few pieces of the spring onions (scallions).

2 Heat the oil in a preheated wok, and lightly scramble the eggs.

3 Add the rice and stir to make sure that each grain of rice is separated. Add the remaining salt, spring onions (scallions) and the peas. Blend well and serve.

# PORK DUMPLINGS

*Jiao Zi*

These dumplings make a good starter to a multi-course meal when shallow-fried. They can also be served on their own as a snack, if steamed, or as a complete meal when poached in large quantities.

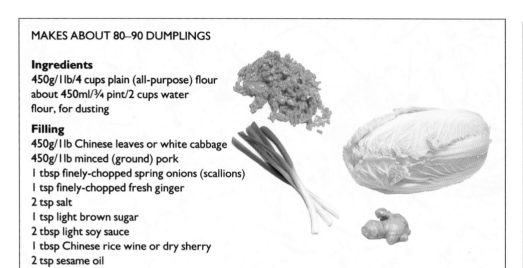

## MAKES ABOUT 80–90 DUMPLINGS

### Ingredients
450g/1lb/4 cups plain (all-purpose) flour
about 450ml/¾ pint/2 cups water
flour, for dusting

### Filling
450g/1lb Chinese leaves or white cabbage
450g/1lb minced (ground) pork
1 tbsp finely-chopped spring onions (scallions)
1 tsp finely-chopped fresh ginger
2 tsp salt
1 tsp light brown sugar
2 tbsp light soy sauce
1 tbsp Chinese rice wine or dry sherry
2 tsp sesame oil

### Dip Sauce

2 tbsp red chilli oil
1 tbsp light soy sauce
1 tsp finely-chopped garlic
1 tbsp finely-chopped spring onions (scallions)

Combine all the ingredients in a small bowl, and serve with Pork Dumplings.

**1** Sift the flour into a bowl, then slowly pour in the water and mix to a firm dough. Knead until smooth and soft, then cover with a damp cloth and set aside for 25–30 minutes.

**2** For the filling, blanch the cabbage leaves until soft. Drain and finely chop. Mix the cabbage with the remaining ingredients

**3** Lightly dust a work surface with the flour. Knead and roll the dough into a long sausage about 2.5cm/1in in diameter. Cut the sausage into about 80–90 small pieces and flatten each piece with the palm of your hand.

**4** Using a rolling pin, roll out each piece into a thin pancake about 6cm/2.5in in diameter.

**5** Place about 1½ tbsp of the filling in the centre of each pancake and fold into a half-moon-shaped pouch.

**6** Pinch the edges firmly so that the dumpling is tightly sealed.

**Shallow-frying**: Heat 3 tbsp of oil in a wok or frying pan. Place the dumplings in rows in the oil and fry over a medium heat for 2–3 minutes.

**Steaming**: Place the dumplings on a bed of lettuce leaves on the rack of a bamboo steamer and steam for 10–12 minutes on a high heat. Serve hot with a dip sauce.

**Poaching**: Cook the dumplings in about 150ml/¼ pint/⅔ cup salted boiling water for 2 minutes. Remove from the heat, and leave the dumplings in the water for about 15 minutes.

# SPECIAL FRIED RICE

*Yangchow Chao Fan*

Special Fried Rice is more elaborate than Egg Fried Rice, and almost a meal in itself.

**SERVES 4**

**Ingredients**
50g/2oz peeled and cooked prawns (shrimp)
50g/2oz cooked ham
115g/4oz green peas
3 eggs

1 tsp salt
2 spring onions (scallions), finely chopped
4 tbsp vegetable oil
1 tbsp light soy sauce
1 tbsp Chinese rice wine or dry sherry
450g/1lb cooked rice

1 Pat dry the prawns (shrimp) with absorbent paper. Cut the ham into small dice about the same size as the peas.

2 In a bowl, lightly beat the eggs with a pinch of the salt and a few pieces of the spring onions (scallions).

3 Heat about half of the oil in a preheated wok, stir-fry the peas, prawns (shrimp) and ham for 1 minute, then add the soy sauce and wine or sherry. Remove and keep warm.

4 Heat the remaining oil in the wok and lightly scramble the eggs. Add the rice and stir to make sure that each grain of rice is separated. Add the remaining salt, spring onions (scallions) and the prawns (shrimp), ham and peas. Blend well and serve either hot or cold.

# WONTON SOUP

*Wun Tun Tang*

In China, wonton soup is served as a snack or Dim Sum rather than as a soup course during a large meal.

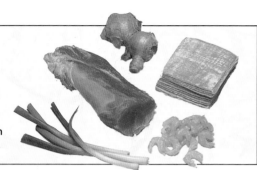

**SERVES 4**

**Ingredients**
175g/6oz pork, not too lean, coarsely chopped
50g/2oz peeled prawns (shrimp), finely minced (ground)
1 tsp light brown sugar
1 tbsp Chinese rice wine or dry sherry

1 tbsp light soy sauce
1 tsp finely-chopped spring onions (scallions)
1 tsp finely-chopped fresh ginger
24 ready-made wonton skins
about 700ml/1 ¼ pints/3 cups Basic Stock
1 tbsp light soy sauce
finely-chopped spring onions (scallions), to garnish

1 In a bowl, mix the pork and prawns (shrimp) with the sugar, wine or sherry, soy sauce, spring onions (scallions) and ginger. Blend well and leave to stand for 25–30 minutes.

2 Place about 1 tsp of the filling at the centre of each wonton skin.

3 Wet and join the edges of each wonton, pressing down with your fingers to seal, then fold each wonton over.

4 To cook, bring the stock to a rolling boil in a wok or saucepan, add the wontons and cook for 4–5 minutes. Season with the soy sauce and garnish with the spring onions (scallions). Serve.

# SEAFOOD CHOW MEIN

## *Hai Wei Chao Mein*

### This basic recipe can be adapted using different items for the 'dressing'.

**SERVES 4**

**Ingredients**
85g/3oz squid, cleaned
85g/3oz uncooked prawns (shrimp)
3–4 fresh scallops
½ egg white
1 tbsp cornflour (cornstarch) paste
250g/9oz egg noodles
5–6 tbsp vegetable oil
50g/2oz mange-tout (snow peas)
½ tsp salt

½ tsp light brown sugar
1 tbsp Chinese rice wine or dry sherry
2 tbsp light soy sauce
2 spring onions (scallions), finely shredded
Basic Stock, if necessary
few drops sesame oil

1 Open up the squid and, using a sharp knife, score the inside in a criss-cross pattern. Cut the squid into pieces each about the size of a postage stamp. Soak the squid in a bowl of boiling water until all the pieces curl up. Rinse in cold water and drain.

2 Peel the prawns (shrimp) and cut each in half lengthways.

3 Cut each scallop into 3–4 slices. Mix the scallops and prawns (shrimp) with the egg white and cornflour (cornstarch) paste.

4 Cook the noodles in boiling water according to the instructions on the packet, then drain and rinse under cold water. Mix with about 1 tbsp of the oil.

5 Heat about 2–3 tbsp of the oil in a wok until hot. Stir-fry the mange-tout (snow peas) and seafood for about 2 minutes then add the salt, sugar, wine or sherry, half of the soy sauce and about half of the spring onions (scallions); blend well and add a little stock, if necessary. Remove and keep warm.

6 Heat the remaining oil in the wok and stir-fry the noodles for 2–3 minutes with the remaining soy sauce. Place in a large serving dish, pour the 'dressing' on top, garnish with the remaining spring onions (scallions) and sprinkle with sesame oil. Serve hot or cold.

*Qing Cai Chao Ji Si*, **50**
*Qing Tang*, **22**
*Qing Zheng Yu*, **39**

Red and white prawns with green vegetable, **40**
Red bean paste, **9**
    red bean paste pancakes, **88**
Rice
    egg fried rice, **76**
    Malacca fried rice, **86**
    plain rice, **76**
    special fried rice, **80**
Rice vinegar, **9**
Rice wine, **9**
Rock sugar, **9**
*Rou Pian Chao Shucai*, **58, 61**

*San Xian Tang*, **28**
Sand-pot, **8**
Scallions. *See* Spring onions
Scallops
    fried seafood with vegetables, **30**
    seafood chow mien, **82**
Seafood
    fried seafood with vegetables, **30**
    seafood chow mien, **82**
Sesame oil, **9**
Sesame sauce
    bon-bon chicken with sesame sauce, **14**
Sesame seed shrimp toasts, **16**
*Shi Zi Tou*, **58**
Shiitake
    hot and sour soup, **23**
Shredded chicken with celery, **50**
Shrimp. *See* Prawns
Shrimps
    sesame seed shrimp toasts, **16**
Sichuan peppercorns, **9**
Sichuan spicy bean curd, **68**
Sichuan yu-hsiang aubergine in spicy sauce, **69**
Sliced fish and coriander soup, **26**
Soup
    chicken and asparagus soup, **25**
    hot and sour soup, **23**
    lamb and cucumber soup, **28**
    noodles in soup, **74**
    pork and noodle broth with prawns, **84**
    sliced fish and coriander soup, **26**
    spinach and bean curd soup, **26**
    sweetcorn and chicken soup, **24**
    sweetcorn and crabmeat soup, **24**
    three-delicacy soup, **28**
    wonton soup, **81**
Soy sauce, **9**
Soy-braised chicken, **52**
Spare-ribs
    basic stock, **22**
    deep-fried spare-ribs with spicy salt and
        pepper, **12**
Special fried rice, **80**
Spinach and bean curd soup, **26**

Spring greens
    crispy 'seaweed', **16**
Spring onions
    baked crab with spring onions and ginger, **43**
    chicken and ham with green vegetables, **54**
    chicken with Chinese vegetables, **50**
    crispy spring rolls, **10**
    fried seafood with vegetables, **30**
    lion's head casserole, **58**
    Malacca fried rice, **86**
    steamed fish with ginger and spring onions,
        **39**
    stir-fried lamb with spring onions, **62**
    stir-fried pork with vegetables, **61**
    stuffed green peppers, **56**
    twice-cooked pork Sichuan style, **57**
Spring rolls
    crab, pork and mushroom spring rolls, **85**
    crispy spring rolls, **10**
Squid
    deep-fried squids with salt and pepper, **13**
    fried seafood with vegetables, **30**
    seafood chowmien, **82**
Steamed fish with ginger and spring onions, **39**
Steamer, **8**
Stir-fried lamb with spring onions, **62**
Stir-fried mixed vegetables, **66**
Stir-fried pork with vegetables, **61**
Stir-fried tomatoes, cucumber and eggs, **72**
Stir-frying, ingredients for, **8**
Stock, basic, **22**
Strainer, **8**
Straw mushrooms, **9**
    beef with Cantonese oyster sauce, **65**
Stuffed green peppers, **56**
*Su Shi Jin*, **66**
*Suan La Tang*, **23**
Sweet and sour
    deep-fried wonton skins with sweet and sour
        sauce, **15**
    pickled sweet and sour cucumber, **18**
    sweet and sour lamb, **62**
    sweet and sour pork, **60**
    sweet and sour prawns, **34**
Sweetcorn
    baby corn cobs, **8**
    beef with Cantonese oyster sauce, **65**
    stir-fried mixed vegetables II, **66**
    sweetcorn and chicken soup, **24**
    sweetcorn and crabmeat soup, **24**

*Tan Chu Huang Gua*, **18**
*Tang Cu Gu Luo Rou*, **60**
*Tang Cu Xia*, **34**
*Tang Cu Yang Rou*, **62**
*Tang mein*, **74**
Thin pancakes, **88**
Three-delicacy soup, **28**
Toffee apple, **90**
Tofu. *See* Bean curd
Tomatoes

chicken wonton soup with prawn, tomato
    and cucumber, **86**
pork with vegetables, **58**
stir-fried tomatoes, cucumbers and eggs, **72**
Twice-cooked pork Sichuan style, **57**

Vegetables
    chicken and ham with green vegetables, **53**
    chicken with Chinese vegetables, **50**
    fried seafood with vegetables, **30**
    pork with vegetables, **58**
    stir-fried mixed vegetables, **66**
    stir-fried pork with vegetables, **61**

Water chestnuts, **9**
    stuffed green peppers, **56**
Wok, **8**
Wonton
    chicken wonton soup with prawn, tomato
        and cucumber, **86**
    deep-fried wonton skins with sweet and sour
        sauce, **15**
    skins, **9**
    wonton soup, **81**
Wood-ears, **9**
    mu-shu pork with eggs and wood-ears, **54**
*Wun Tun Tang*, **81**

*Xiang Cui Ya*, **44**
*Xie Rou Yumi Tang*, **24**
*Xing Ren Tou Fou*, **91**

*Yang Rou Huang Gua Tang*, **28**
*Yangchow Chao Fan*, **80**
    sweet and sour lamb, **62**
*Yu Hsiang Gai*, **69**
*Yu Pian Yen Hsee Tang*, **26**
*Yuan Yang Xia*, **40**

*Zha Pai Ku*, **12**
*Zha Chu Kuen*, **10**
*Zha Xie*, **43**
Zucchini. *See* Courgettes

Eggplant. *See* Aubergine
Eggs
    egg fried rice, **76**
    fu-yung chicken, **46**
    Malacca fried rice, **86**
    mu-shu pork with eggs and wood-ears, **54**
    prawn fu-yung, **32**
    special fried rice, **80**
    stir-fried tomatoes, cucumbers and eggs, **72**
Equipment and utensils, **8**

*Feng Wei Xia*, **20**
Fish
    braised fish fillet with mushrooms, **32**
    braised whole fish in chilli and garlic sauce, **38**
    sliced fish and coriander soup, **26**
    steamed fish with ginger and spring onions, **39**
Five-spice powder, **9**
Fried seafood with vegetables, **30**
*Fu Ron Ji*, **46**
*Fu Ron Xia*, **32**
Fu-yung
    fu-yung chicken, **46**
    prawn fu-yung, **32**

*Gan Shao Niu Rou*, **64**
*Gan Shao Yu*, **38**
Garlic
    braised whole fish in chilli and garlic sauce, **38**
Ginger
    baked crab with spring onions and ginger, **43**
    steamed fish with ginger and spring onions, **39**
Ginger juice, **13**
Ginger root, **9**

*Hai Wei Chao Mein*, **82**
Ham
    chicken and ham with green vegetables, **53**
    special fried rice, **80**
    three-delicacy soup, **28**
*Hao You Nui Rou*, **65**
HoiSin sauce, **9**
*Hong Dao Guo Ping*, **88**
Hot and sour cabbage, **18**
Hot and sour soup, **23**
*Hsai Jen Tu Ssu*, **16**
*Hui Guo Rou*, **57**

*Ji Pian Chao Shi Cai*, **50**
*Ji Wun Tun*, **86**
*Jiang Cong Guo Long Xia*, **42**
*Jiang You Ji*, **52**
*Jiao Yan You Yu*, **13**
*Jin Hua Yi Shu Ji*, **53**

*Kung Po Ji Ding*, **47**
'Kung-po' chicken Sichuan-style, **47**

Ladle and spatula, **8**
Lamb
    lamb and cucumber soup, **28**
    stir-fried lamb with spring onions, **62**
    sweet and sour lamb, **62**
Leeks
    crispy spring rolls, **10**
Lemon sole
    braised fish fillet with mushrooms, **32**
    sliced fish and coriander soup, **26**
Lion's head casserole, **58**

Lobster
    baked lobster with black beans, **42**
*Lusan Ji Rou Tang*, **25**

Malacca fried rice, **86**
Mange-tout
    beef with Cantonese oyster sauce, **65**
    chicken with Chinese vegetables, **50**
    red and white prawns with green vegetable, **40**
    seafood chow mien, **82**
    stir-fried mixed vegetables I, **66**
    stir-fried pork with vegetables, **61**

*Mu Shu Rou*, **54**
Mu-shu pork with eggs and wood-ears, **54**
Mushrooms
    bamboo shoots and Chinese mushrooms, **72**
    beef with Cantonese oyster sauce, **65**
    braised fish fillet with mushrooms, **32**
    chicken with Chinese vegetables, **50**
    crab, pork and mushroom spring rolls, **85**
    crispy spring rolls, **10**
    dried Chinese mushrooms, **9**
    hot and sour soup, **23**
    lion's head casserole, **58**
    mu-shu pork with eggs and wood-ears, **54**
    noodles in soup, **74**
    stir-fried mixed vegetables I, **66**
    stir-fried pork with vegetables, **61**
    straw, **9**
    wood-ears, **9**

*Niang Qing Chaio*, **56**
Noodles

    noodles in soup, **74**
    pork and noodle broth with prawns, **84**
    seafood chow mien, **82**

Oyster sauce, **9**
    beef with Cantonese oyster sauce, **65**

*Pai Fan*, **76**
Pancakes
    red bean paste pancakes, **88**
    thin pancakes, **88**
*Pao Cai Dao Fu Tang*, **26**
Peas
    Malacca fried rice, **86**
    special fried rice, **80**
Peking duck, **48**
Peppers
    fried seafood with vegetables, **30**
    stir-fried mixed vegetables I, **66**
    stuffed green peppers, **56**
    twice-cooked pork Sichuan style, **57**
*Pho*, **84**
Pickled sweet and sour cucumber, **18**
Plaice
    braised fish fillet with mushrooms, **32**
    sliced fish and coriander soup, **26**
Plum sauce, **9**
Pork
    basic stock, **22**
    crab, pork and mushroom spring rolls, **85**
    deep-fried spare-ribs with spicy salt and pepper, **12**
    hot and sour soup, **23**
    lion's head casserole, **58**
    Malacca fried rice, **86**
    mu-shu pork with eggs and wood-ears, **54**
    noodles in soup, **74**
    pork and noodle broth with prawns, **84**
    pork with vegetables, **58**
    stir-fried pork with vegetables, **61**
    stuffed green peppers, **56**
    sweet and sour pork, **60**
    twice-cooked pork Sichuan style, **57**
    wonton soup, **81**
Prawns
    butterfly prawns, **20**
    chicken wonton soup with prawn, tomato and cucumber, **86**
    fried seafood with vegetables, **30**
    lion's head casserole, **58**
    Malacca fried rice, **86**
    pork and noodle broth with prawns, **84**
    prawn fu-yung, **32**
    red and white prawns with green vegetable, **40**
    seafood chow mien, **82**
    special fried rice, **80**
    stir-fried prawns with broccoli, **35**
    sweet and sour prawns, **34**
    three-delicacy soup, **28**
    wonton soup, **81**

# INDEX

Agar-agar, **8**
   almond curd junket, **91**
Almond curd junket, **91**
Apple, toffee, **90**
Asparagus
   chicken and asparagus soup, **25**
Aubergine
   Sichuan yu-hsiang aubergine in spicy sauce,
    **69**

*Ba Tsu Ping Guo*, **90**
Baked crab with spring onions and ginger, **43**
Baked lobster with black beans, **42**
Bamboo shoots, **8**
   bamboo shoots and Chinese mushrooms, **72**
   chicken with Chinese vegetables, **50**
   hot and sour soup, **23**
   mu-shu pork with eggs and wood-ears, **54**
   sweet and sour pork, **60**
   twice-cooked pork Sichuan style, **57**

*Bao Bing*, **88**
Basic stock, **22**
Bean curd, **8**
   Sichuan spicy bean curd, **68**
   spinach and bean curd soup, **26**
Bean sprouts, **8**
   crispy spring rolls, **10**
Beef
   beef with Cantonese oyster sauce, **65**
   deep-fried shredded beef, **64**
   Sichuan spicy bean curd, **68**
*Bei Jing Ya*, **48**
Black bean sauce, **8**
   baked lobster with black beans, **42**
   Sichuan spicy bean curd, **68**
Black beans, salted, **9**
Bon-bon chicken with sesame sauce, **14**
*Bon Bon Ji*, **14**
Braised fish fillet with mushrooms, **32**
Braised whole fish in chilli and garlic sauce, **38**
Broccoli
   chicken and ham with green vegetables, **53**
   stir-fried mixed vegetables II, **66**
   stir-fried prawns with broccoli, **35**
Butterfly prawns, **20**

Cabbage
   hot and sour cabbage, **18**
*Cai Sung*, **16**
Carrots
   crispy spring rolls, **10**
   deep-fried shredded beef, **64**
   fried seafood with vegetables, **30**
   stir-fried mixed vegetables II, **66**
   stir-fried pork with vegetables, **61**
Celery
   dry-fried shredded beef, **64**
   fried seafood with vegetables, **30**
   shredded chicken with celery, **50**
*Cha Gio*, **85**
*Cha Won Tun*, **15**
*Chao San Wei*, **72**
*Chao San Xian*, **30**
*Chao Shang Dong*, **72**
Chicken
   basic stock, **22**
   bon-bon chicken with sesame sauce, **14**
   chicken and asparagus soup, **25**
   chicken and ham with green vegetables, **53**
   chicken with Chinese vegetables, **50**
   chicken wonton soup with prawn, tomato
    and cucumber, **86**
   fu-yung chicken, **46**
   hot and sour soup, **23**
   'kung-po' chicken Sichuan-style, **47**
   noodles in soup, **74**
   shredded chicken with celery, **50**
   soy-braised chicken, **52**
   sweetcorn and chicken soup, **24**
   three-delicacy soup, **28**
Chilli bean sauce, **8**
   braised whole fish in chilli and garlic sauce,
    **38**
Chilli oil, **8**
Chilli sauce, **8, 9**
*Chin Chao Yu Tiao*, **32**
Chinese cleaver, **8**
Chinese cooking
   equipment and utensils, **8**
   ingredients, **8, 9**
   principles of, **8**
Chinese leaves, **9**
   lion's head casserole, **58**
Chinese mushrooms
   bamboo shoots and Chinese mushrooms, **72**
   chicken with Chinese vegetables, **50**
   crab, pork and mushroom spring rolls, **85**
   hot and sour soup, **23**
Chinese leaves
   mu-shu pork with eggs and wood-ears, **54**
   stir-fried mixed vegetables II, **66**
*Chow fan*, **86**

*Ci lan Chao Xia Ren*, **35**
*Cong Bao Yang Rou*, **62**
Coriander, **9**
   sliced fish and coriander soup, **26**
Cornflour paste, **10**
Cornstarch paste, **10**
Courgettes
   pork with vegetables, **58**
   stir-fried mixed vegetables I, **66**
Crab
   baked crab with spring onions and ginger, **43**
   crab, pork and mushroom spring rolls, **85**
Crispy 'seaweed', **16**
Crispy and aromatic duck, **44**
Crispy spring rolls, **10**
Cucumber
   chicken wonton soup with prawn, tomato
    and cucumber, **86**
   lamb and cucumber soup, **28**
   pickled sweet and sour cucumber, **18**
   stir-fried tomatoes, cucumbers and eggs, **72**

Dry-fried shredded beef, **64**
Deep-fried spare-ribs with spicy salt and
   pepper, **12**
Deep-fried squids with salt and pepper, **13**
Deep-fried wonton skins with sweet and sour
   sauce, **15**
Desserts
   almond curd junket, **91**
   red bean paste pancakes, **88**
   thin pancakes, **88**
   toffee apple, **90**

Dried Chinese mushrooms, **9**
   noodles in soup, **74**
Duck
   crispy and aromatic duck, **44**
   Peking duck, **48**
Duck pancakes, **88**
Duck sauce, **48**
*Dun Chao Fan*, **76**

Egg noodles, **9**
   noodles in soup, **74**
   pork and noodles broth with prawns, **84**
   seafood chow mein, **82**

## Canada

**Dah'ls Oriental Food** 822 Broadview, Toronto, Ontario, M4K 2P7, (416) 463-8109

**Hong Kong Emporium** 364 Young Street, Toronto, Ontario, M5B 1S5, (416) 977-3386

**U-Can-Buy Oriental Food** 5692 Victoria Avenue, Montreal, Quebec, H3W 2P8

## Australia

**Korean, Japanese and Oriental Food Store** 14 Oxford Street, Sydney 2000

**Oriental Import** 406a Brighton Road, Brighton, South Australia

## New Zealand

**Chinese Food Centre** Davis Trading Company Ltd, Te Puni Street, Petone, 568-2009

## South Africa

**Akhalwaya and Sons** Gillies Street, Burgersdorp, Johannesburg, (11) 838-1008

**Kashmiris Spice Centre** 95 Church Street, Mayfair, Johannesburg, (11) 839-3883

**Haribak and Sons Ltd** 31 Pine Street, Durban (31) 32-662

**Spice Emporium** 31 Pine Street, Durban, (31) 32 662

# ACKNOWLEDGEMENTS

The authors and publishers would like to thank the following for generously supplying food products and equipment:

B E International Foods Limited
Grafton House
Stockingswater Lane
Enfield
Middlesex EN3

Cherry Valley Farms Ltd
Rotherwell, Lincoln

Wing Yip
395 Edgware Road
London NW2

# STOCKISTS AND SUPPLIERS

## United Kingdom

### Birmingham
**Wing Yip** 375 Nechells Park Road, Nechells, Birmingham B7 5NT
(021) 327-6618

**Janson Hong** St Martins House, 17–18 Bull Ring, Birmingham B5 5DD
(021) 643-4681

### Leeds
**Wing Lee Hong** 6 Edward Street, Leeds LS2 7NN
(0532) 457203

### Liverpool
**Chung Wah** 31–32 Great George Square, Liverpool L1 5DZ
(051) 709-2637

**Hondo** 5–11 Upper Duke Street, Liverpool L1 9DU
(051) 708-5409

### London
**Wing Yip** 395 Edgware Road, Cricklewood, London NW2 6LN
(081) 450-0422

**Loon Fung** 42–44 Gerrard Street, London W1V 7LP
(071) 437-7332

**Loon Moon** 9a Gerrard Street, London W1V 7LJ
(071) 734-9940

**See Woo Supermarket** 18–20 Lisle Street, London WC2
(071) 439-8325

### Manchester
**Wing Yip** Oldham Road, Ancoats, Manchester M8 4BA
(061) 832-3215

**Wing Fat** 49 Faulkner Street, Manchester M1 4EE
(061) 236-0788

### Newcastle
**Eastern Pearl** 27–31 Fenkle Street, Newcastle-upon-Tyne NE1 5XN
(091) 261-5623

### Oxford
**Lung Wah Chong** 41–42 Hythe Bridge Street, Oxford OX1 2EP
(0865) 790703

### Portsmouth
**Sun Hun Chan** 6 Tricorn Shopping Centre, Portsmouth, Hants PO1 4AE
(0705) 812487

## United States

### Arizona
**G&L Import-Export Corp.** 4828 East 22nd Street, Tuscon, Arizona, 85706
(602) 790-9016

**Manila Oriental Foodmart** 3557 West Dunlap Avenue, Phoenix, Arizona, 85021
(602) 841-2977

### California
**Chinese Grocer** 209 Post Street, San Francisco, California, 94108
(415) 982-0125

**Good Earth Seed Co.** P.O. Box 5644, Redwood City, California, 94603
(415) 595-2270

**Shing Chong & Company** 800 Grand Avenue, San Francisco, California, 94108
(415) 982-0949

### Illinois
**Bankok Oriental Grocery** 7430 Harlem Avenue, Bridgeview, Illinois 60455
(708) 458-1810

**Chang Oriental Foods** 5214 North Lincoln Avenue, Chicago, Illinois, 60646
(312) 271-5050

### Massachusetts
**Chung Wah Hong Co.** 55 Beach Street, Boston, Massachusetts, 02111
(617) 426-3619

**See Sun Co.** 25 Harrison Avenue, Boston, Massachusetts, 02111
(617) 426-0954

### New Jersey
**Chinese Kitchen** P.O. Box 218, Stirling, New Jersey, 07980
(201) 665-2234

### New York
**Eastern Trading Co.** 2801 Broadway, New York, New York, 10025

**The Oriental Country Store** 12 Mott Street, New York, New York, 10013

**Wing Fat Co.** 35 Mott Street, New York, New York, 10013

### Ohio
**Crestview Market** 200 Crestview Road, Columbus, Ohio, 43202
(614) 267-2723

# ALMOND CURD JUNKET

*Xing Ren Tou Fou*

Also known as Almond Float, this is usually made from agar-agar or isinglass, though gelatine can also be used.

SERVES 4–6

**Ingredients**
7g/¼oz agar-agar or isinglass or 25g/1oz
　gelatine powder
about 575ml/1 pint/2½ cups water
4 tbsp granulated or caster (superfine) sugar

300ml/½ pint/1¼ cups milk
1 tsp almond essence (extract)
fresh or canned mixed fruit salad with syrup, to
　serve

1 In a saucepan, dissolve the agar-agar or isinglass in about half of the water over a gentle heat. This will take at least 10 minutes. If using gelatine, follow the instructions.

2 In a separate saucepan, dissolve the sugar in the remaining water over a medium heat. Add the milk and the almond essence (extract), blending well, but do not boil.

3 Mix the milk and sugar with the agar-agar or isinglass mixture in a large serving bowl. When cool, place in the refrigerator for 2–3 hours to set.

4 To serve, cut the 'junket' into small cubes and spoon into a serving dish or into individual bowls. Pour the fruit salad, with the syrup, over the junket and serve.

# TOFFEE APPLES

*Ba Tsu Ping Guo*

A variety of fruits, such as banana and pineapple, can be prepared and cooked the same way.

**SERVES 4**

**Ingredients**
4 firm eating apples, peeled and cored
115g/4oz/1 cup plain (all-purpose) flour
about 100ml/4fl oz/½ cup cold water
1 egg, beaten

vegetable oil, for deep-frying, plus 2 tbsp for the
    toffee
115g/4oz/½ cup granulated or caster (superfine)
    sugar

1 Cut each apple into 8 pieces. Dust each
piece with a little of the flour.

2 Sift the remaining flour into a mixing
bowl, then slowly add the cold water and
stir to make a smooth batter. Add the beaten
egg and blend well.

3 Heat the oil in a wok. Dip the apple
pieces in the batter and deep-fry for about
3 minutes or until golden. Remove and drain.

4 Heat 2 tbsp of the oil in the wok, add the
sugar and stir continuously until the sugar
has caramelized. Quickly add the apple pieces
and blend well so that each piece of apple is
coated with the 'toffee'. Dip the apple pieces in
cold water to harden before serving.

# THIN PANCAKES

### *Bao Bing*

Thin pancakes are not too difficult to make, but quite a lot of practice and patience is needed to achieve the perfect result. Nowadays, even restaurants buy frozen ready-made ones from Chinese supermarkets. If you decide to use ready-made pancakes, or are reheating home-made ones, steam them for about 5 minutes, or microwave on high (650 watts) for 1–2 minutes.

MAKES 24–30

**Ingredients**
450g/1lb/4 cups plain (all-purpose) flour

about 300ml/½ pint/1¼ cups boiling water
1 tsp vegetable oil
flour, for dusting

*Cook's tip*

Cooked pancakes can be stored in the refrigerator for several days.

1 Sift the flour into a mixing bowl, then pour in the boiling water very gently, stirring as you pour. Mix with the oil and knead the mixture into a firm dough. Cover with a damp towel and let stand for about 30 minutes. Lightly dust a work surface with flour.

2 Knead the dough for about 5–8 minutes or until smooth, then divide it into 3 equal portions. Roll out each portion into a long 'sausage', cut each into 8–10 pieces and roll each into a ball. Using your palm, press each piece into a flat pancake. With a rolling pin, gently roll each into a 15cm/6in circle.

3 Heat an ungreased frying pan until hot, then reduce the heat to low and place the pancakes, one at a time, in the pan. Remove the pancakes when small brown spots appear on the underside. Keep under a damp cloth until all the pancakes are cooked.

# RED BEAN PASTE PANCAKES

### *Hong Dao Guo Ping*

If you are unable to find red bean paste, sweetened chestnut purée or mashed dates are possible substitutes.

SERVES 4

**Ingredients**
about 8 tbsp sweetened red bean paste

8 Thin Pancakes
2–3 tbsp vegetable oil
granulated or caster (superfine) sugar, to serve

1 Spread about 1 tbsp of the red bean paste over about three-quarters of each pancake, then roll each pancake over three or four times.

2 Heat the oil in a wok or frying pan and shallow-fry the pancake rolls until golden brown, turning once.

3 Cut each pancake roll into 3–4 pieces and sprinkle with sugar to serve.

# CHICKEN WONTON SOUP WITH PRAWNS (SHRIMP)

*Ji Wun Tun Tang*

This soup is a more luxurious version of basic Wonton Soup, and is almost a meal in itself.

SERVES 4

**Ingredients**
325g/11oz chicken breast fillet, skin removed
200g/7oz prawn (shrimp) tails, fresh or cooked
1 tsp finely-chopped fresh ginger

2 spring onions (scallions), finely chopped
1 egg
2 tsp oyster sauce (optional)
salt and pepper
1 packet wonton skins
1 tbsp cornflour (cornstarch) paste

850ml/1½ pints/3¾ cups chicken stock
¼ cucumber, peeled and diced
1 spring onion (scallion), roughly shredded, to garnish
4 sprigs coriander leaves, to garnish
1 tomato, skinned, seeded and diced, to garnish

1 Place the chicken breast, 150g/5oz prawn (shrimp) tails, ginger and spring onions (scallions) in a food processor and mix for 2–3 minutes. Add the egg, oyster sauce and seasoning and process briefly. Set aside.

2 Place 8 wonton skins at a time on a surface, moisten the edges with flour paste and place ½ tsp of the filling in the centre of each. Fold in half and pinch to seal. Simmer in salted water for 4 minutes.

3 Bring the chicken stock to the boil, add the remaining prawn (shrimp) tails and the cucumber and simmer for 3–4 minutes. Add the wontons and simmer to warm through. Garnish and serve hot.

# MALACCA FRIED RICE

*Chow Fan*

There are many versions of this dish throughout the East, all of which make use of left-over rice. Ingredients vary according to what is available, but prawns (shrimp) are a popular addition.

SERVES 4–6

**Ingredients**
2 eggs
salt and pepper
3 tbsp vegetable oil

4 shallots or 1 medium onion, finely chopped
1 tsp finely-chopped fresh ginger
1 clove garlic, crushed
225g/8oz prawn (shrimp) tails, fresh or cooked
1–2 tsp chilli sauce (optional)
3 spring onions (scallions), green part only,

roughly chopped
225g/8oz frozen peas
225g/8oz thickly sliced roast pork, diced
3 tbsp light soy sauce
350g/12oz long grain rice, cooked

1 In a bowl, beat the eggs well, and season. Heat 1 tbsp of the oil in a large non-stick frying pan, pour in the eggs and allow to set without stirring for less than a minute. Roll up the pancake, cut into thin strips and set aside.

2 Heat the remaining vegetable oil in a large wok, add the shallots, ginger, garlic and prawn (shrimp) tails and cook for 1–2 minutes, ensuring that the garlic doesn't burn.

3 Add the chilli sauce, spring onions (scallions), peas, pork and soy sauce. Stir to heat through, then add the rice. Fry the rice over a moderate heat for 6–8 minutes. Turn into a dish and decorate with the pancake.

# CRAB, PORK AND MUSHROOM SPRING ROLLS

*Cha Gio*

If you cannot obtain minced (ground) pork, use the meat from the equivalent weight of best-quality pork sausages.
Filled spring rolls can be made in advance and kept in the refrigerator ready for frying.

MAKES 12 ROLLS

**Ingredients**
25g/1oz rice noodles
50g/2oz Chinese mushrooms (shiitake), fresh or
   dried
1 tbsp vegetable oil
4 spring onions (scallions), chopped
1 small carrot, grated
175g/6oz minced (ground) pork

100g/4oz/1 cup white crabmeat
1 tsp fish sauce (optional)
salt and pepper
12 frozen spring roll skins, defrosted
2 tbsp cornflour (cornstarch) paste
vegetable oil, for deep-frying
1 head iceberg or bib lettuce, to serve
1 bunch mint or basil, to serve
1 bunch coriander leaves, to serve
½ cucumber, sliced, to serve

1 Bring a large saucepan of salted water to the boil, and simmer the noodles for 8 minutes. Cut the noodles into finger-length pieces. If the mushrooms are dried, soak them in boiling water for 10 minutes before slicing thinly.

2 To make the filling, heat the oil in a wok or frying pan, add the spring onions (scallions), carrot and pork and cook for 8–10 minutes. Remove from the heat, then add the crabmeat, fish sauce and seasoning. Add the noodles and mushrooms, and set aside.

3 To fill the rolls, brush one spring roll skin at a time with the cornflour (cornstarch) paste, then place 1 tsp of the filling onto the skin. Fold the edges towards the middle and roll evenly to make a neat cigar shape. The paste will help seal the wrapper.

4 Heat the oil in a wok or deep-fryer until hot. Fry the spring rolls two at a time in the oil for 6–8 minutes. Make sure the fat is not too hot or the mixture inside will not heat through properly. Serve on a bed of salad leaves, mint, coriander and cucumber.

# PORK AND NOODLE BROTH WITH PRAWNS (SHRIMP)

*Pho*

This quick and delicious recipe can be made with 200g/7oz boneless chicken breast instead of pork fillet.

### SERVES 4–6

**Ingredients**
350g/12oz pork chops or 200g/7oz pork fillet
225g/8oz fresh prawn (shrimp) tails or cooked
    prawns (shrimp)
150g/5oz thin egg noodles
1 tbsp vegetable oil
2 tsp sesame oil
4 shallots, or 1 medium onion, sliced
1 tbsp fresh ginger, finely sliced

1 clove garlic, crushed
1 tsp granulated sugar
1.4 litres/2½ pints/6¼ cups chicken stock
2 lime leaves
3 tbsp fish sauce
juice of ½ lime
4 sprigs coriander leaves, to garnish
chopped green part of 2 spring onions (scallions),
    to garnish

1 If using pork chops, trim away fat and bone completely. Place the meat in the freezer for 30 minutes to firm but not freeze the meat. Slice the meat thinly and set aside. Peel and de-vein the prawns (shrimp), if fresh.

2 Bring a large saucepan of salted water to the boil and simmer the noodles for the time stated on the packet. Drain and refresh under cold running water. Set aside.

3 Heat the vegetable and sesame oils in a large saucepan, add the shallots and brown evenly, for 3–4 minutes. Remove from the pan and set aside.

4 Add the ginger, garlic, sugar and chicken stock and bring to a simmer with the lime leaves. Add the fish sauce and lime juice. Add the pork, then simmer for 15 minutes. Add the prawns and noodles and simmer for 3–4 minutes. Serve in shallow soup bowls and decorate with the coriander leaves, the green part of the spring onions (scallions) and the browned shallots.